THE
COCKNEY
RHYMING
SLANG
DICTIONARY

T0275438

To my bread knife
and two bottles of water

THE
COCKNEY
RHYMING
SLANG
DICTIONARY

GEOFF
TIBBALLS

POP PRESS

Contents

Introduction

If you ask someone outside London whether they regularly use Cockney rhyming slang, they might answer, 'Not on your Nellie!' – blissfully unaware that 'not on your Nellie' is itself a derivative of Cockney rhyming slang, from 'Nellie Duff' meaning 'puff', which is slang for 'life'. So 'not on your Nellie' means 'not on your life'.

The first mention of rhyming slang is in John Camden Hotten's 1859 book *The Slang Dictionary* and the popularly held belief is that it was designed by criminals and shady street sellers as a secret code indecipherable to outsiders, especially the police. Over the next 100 years it was adopted by working-class Cockneys in general – often to provide euphemisms for embarrassing conditions or situations.

On the following pages you will find rhymes old and new, popular and obscure, and like any self-respecting dictionary there are translations from Cockney to English and vice versa. So if you want to know the contributions that such diverse characters as Sebastian Coe, Vera Lynn and Noddy Holder have made to the language, the meaning of quaint phrases like 'Oi Jimmy Knacker' and 'tumble down the sink', the answers are all in this, the ultimate Captain Hook about Chitty Chitty Bang Bang.

Geoff Tibballs

Cockney to English

A

Adam and Eve believe
(One of the most familiar rhyming slang terms, dating from the late nineteenth century, as in, 'Would you Adam and Eve it, he's run off with my skin and blister!')

Adam Ants pants

Air Force sauce

Air gunner stunner

Airs and graces Epsom races, braces
(In the 1900s this term referred to Epsom races but it subsequently changed to mean the elastic straps that held up men's trousers.)

Ajax tax
(From the powerful household cleaner introduced in 1947 with the jingle: 'You'll stop paying the elbow tax/When you start cleaning with Ajax'.)

Alan Whickers knickers
(British TV personality famous for being lampooned on *Monty Python*'s 'Whicker Island'. Usually shortened to 'Alans', as in the 1998 film *Lock, Stock and Two Smoking Barrels* when Nick the Greek says: 'Alright, alright, keep your Alans on!')

Alderman's nail tail
(As in the expression 'as happy as a dog with two aldermen'.)

Alexander the Great plate

(After the king of Macedonia (356–323 BC) who spectacularly expanded his empire during his short life.)

Alfred the Great weight
(After the ninth-century King of Wessex.)

Alligator later
(As in 'see you later, alligator' – with its response of 'in a while, crocodile'.)

Almond rocks socks

Andy Pandy shandy
(First appearing in 1950, stringed puppet Andy Pandy appeared on *Watch With Mother* to the delight of thousands of pre-school children. (See also **Looby Loos**.))

Apple fritter bitter (beer)

Apple pips lips

Apples and pears stairs
(This phrase has its origins in the nineteenth century when market-stall holders would arrange their fruit in steps (or 'stairs') with the shiniest apples and pears at the front.)

April Fools tools, football pools
(This was originally an underworld term for a burglar's tools but it was later extended to embrace the craze for doing the football pools that took off in Britain in the 1930s.)

April showers flowers
(This probably stems from the verse 'April showers bring forth May flowers'.)

Aristotle bottle

Armitage Shank bank
(From toilet manufacturers Armitage Shanks.)

Army and Navy gravy

Ascot races braces
(Usually shortened to 'Ascots'.)

Attila the Hun a 2:1 degree result
(The fearsome king of the Huns (406–453) who died on his wedding night is fondly remembered by students, as in, 'Congratulations on getting an Attila; I only got a Desmond'.)

Auntie Ella umbrella

Auntie Nelly belly

B

Baa lamb tram
(Electric baa lambs ran in London from 1901 to 1952 before being reintroduced in Croydon in 2000.)

Babbling brook cook, crook

Baby's pram jam

Backseat driver skiver

Bacon and eggs legs

Bacon rind mind

Bag of sand grand (£1,000)

Bag of yeast priest

Baked bean Queen (Elizabeth II)

Baked beans jeans
(Jeans were originally worn by cowboys, so this rhyme dating from the 1960s might spring from the association between a cowboy's favourite clothing and his favourite food.)

Baker's dozen cousin

(Medieval English bakers would add an extra loaf when selling a dozen in order to avoid being fined under the terms of the Assize of Bread and Ale for giving short measure.)

Bald head red (snooker ball)
(Applied to the red ball in snooker, even though a bald head looks more like the pink.)

Ball and bat hat
(Popular in England before 1914, after which it was largely replaced by 'Tit for tat'.)

Ball of chalk walk

Ball of lead head
(Used in the British army during the First World War but now obsolete.)

Ballet dancer chancer

Balloon car saloon bar

Balmy breeze cheese

Band of Hope soap
(The Band of Hope was a British temperance society formed in Leeds in 1847 to educate children on the perils of drink.)

Bangers and mash cash, slash (urinate)

Bar of soap Pope

Barb wired tired

Barge and tug mug (drinking)

Bark and growl trowel

Barnaby Rudge judge
(A historical novel by Charles Dickens, published in 1841 and dealing in part with the pitfalls of capital punishment. (See also **Dolly Varden**.))

Barnet Fair hair
(The history of Barnet Fair dates back to 1588 when Queen Elizabeth I granted a charter to the Lord of the Manor of Barnet, Charles Butler, for the staging of a twice-yearly fair.)

Basil Fawlty Balti
(After the Torquay hotelier played by John Cleese in the classic 1970s sitcom Fawlty Towers.)

Bat and wicket ticket

Bath bun son, sun

Battle cruiser boozer (pub)
(First heard in the 1940s. Barfly Jack in the 1998 gangster film *Lock, Stock and Two Smoking Barrels*, says: 'He's gone down the battle cruiser to watch the end of a football game'.)

Battle of Waterloo stew
(The Duke of Wellington's finest hour certainly left Napoleon in a stew.)

Beano and Dandy shandy
(The use of two children's comics in the rhyme underlines the belief that shandy is not a drink for real men.)

Beans on toast post

Bear's paw saw

Bees and honey money
(First recorded in 1892, the phrase may be comparing the industry of bees and humans, i.e. bees work hard to produce honey and if humans work hard, they earn money.)

Bees' wax tax

Beggar My Neighbour on the labour (exchange)
(The card game Beggar My Neighbour dates back to at least the mid-nineteenth century, having appeared in Charles Dickens's *Great Expectations* (1861).)

Bell ringers fingers

Benny Hill till, drill
(The association with 'till' is particularly fitting as comedian Benny Hill (1926–92) was famously careful with money.)

Bernie Flint skint
(An alternative to 'boracic lint' from the mid-1970s when singer/guitarist Bernie Flint won the ITV talent show *Opportunity Knocks* a record twelve times.)

Bessie Braddock haddock
(A former Labour MP for a Liverpool constituency, Bessie Braddock (1899–1970) was a big name in English politics after the Second World War.)

Bethnal Greens jeans
(From the area of East London, as in, 'Isn't it about time you bought a new pair of Bethnals?')

Betty Grable table
(US film star Betty Grable (1916–73) was famed for her shapely legs, which were insured for one million dollars.)

Biffo the Bear hair
(Biffo the Bear made his debut in the *Beano* comic in 1948 and occupied the front cover until 1974 when he was ousted by Dennis the Menace.)

Big bass drum bum (bottom)

Big Ben ten

Big dippers slippers

Big Ears and Noddy body
(Big Ears the bearded gnome and Noddy were created by English writer Enid Blyton and first appeared in print in 1949.)

Bill and Ben ten
(Bill and Ben the Flowerpot Men were big hitters in 1950s children's television.)

Bill Oddie and Ben voddie (vodka)

Bill Stickers knickers
(Everyone's favourite victim from the omnipresent warning on walls or hoardings: 'Bill Stickers will be prosecuted'.)

Billy Bunter punter
(Created by Frank Richards, Billy Bunter of Greyfriars School was a popular character in the boys' weekly magazine *The Magnet*, which was published from 1908 to 1940.)

Billy Button mutton
(The rhyme first appeared in the nineteenth century when 'Billy Button' was slang for an itinerant tailor.)

Billy Liar tyre
(The title of a 1959 novel by Keith Waterhouse, the story of 19-year-old undertaker's clerk Billy Fisher and his Walter Mitty-like fantasies.)

Bin lid quid (£1)

Birdlime time (prison sentence)
(Originating in the 1850s, it had been contracted to 'bird' by the 1920s. Hence the term 'to do bird' meaning 'to serve a prison sentence'.)

Bird's nest chest
(No doubt because a hairy chest resembles something that a sparrow has built.)

Biscuits and cheese knees

Black and white night

Black Maria fire
('Black Maria' was first heard in nineteenth-century America to describe a police van carrying prisoners.)

Blackadder ladder
(After Rowan Atkinson's social climber in the historical TV comedy that ran from 1983 to 1989.)

Blackpool Tower shower

(From the Lancashire tower (inspired by Paris's Eiffel Tower) that was completed in 1894.)

Blackwall Tunnel funnel
(After the tunnel under the Thames that opened in 1897. Seven people were killed during its construction.)

Blindman's buff snuff
(Blindman's buff is a children's game that dates back 2,000 years to Greece. In Germany it is called 'blind cow'.)

Bloody Mary scary
(Catholic Queen Mary I, who ruled England from 1553 to 1558, earned the nickname 'Bloody Mary' for her ruthless persecution of Protestants.)

Blue moon spoon

Bo Diddley tiddly
(After the American blues singer (1928–2008).)

Bo Peep sleep
(From the nursery rhyme character Little Bo Peep.)

Board and plank Yank

Boat Race face
(The University Boat Race was first staged in 1829 but it was not until after the Second World War that the term caught on as an expression for 'face'.)

Bob Dylan villain
(After the iconic US folk singer who sprang to fame in the 1960s.)

Bobby Moore score (£20)
(After England's World Cup-winning captain of 1966.)

Bodie and Doyle boil (spot)
(Played by Lewis Collins and Martin Shaw respectively, crimefighters Bodie and Doyle were characters in the ITV series *The Professionals*, which ran from 1977 to 1983.)

Boiled beef and carrot claret (blood)
(In boxing 'claret' is a slang term for 'blood', and in rhyming slang that becomes 'boiled beef and carrot' after the Cockney music-hall song 'Boiled Beef And Carrots'.)

Boiler house spouse
(Hence the less than flattering description of 'er indoors as an 'old boiler'.)

Boots and socks pox

Boracic lint skint
(Boracic lint was a form of medical dressing popular in the nineteenth century. Just the word 'boracic' is sufficient to mean 'penniless'. First recorded in 1959.)

Borrow and beg egg
(Used during the Second World War when due to food shortages, eggs could often only be obtained by borrowing or begging.)

Bottle and stopper copper (police officer)

Bottle of beer ear

Bottle of booze news

Bottle of cola bowler (hat)

Bottle of rum bum (bottom)

Bottle of sauce horse

Bottle of Scotch watch

Bottle of water daughter

Bottle of wine fine (penalty)

Bow and arrow sparrow
('Who Killed Cock Robin?' asked the nursery rhyme, first published in 1744. 'I, said the sparrow, with my bow and arrow'. (See also **Sparrow**.))

Bow and quiver liver

Bowl of fruit suit

Bowl the hoop soup
(A favourite children's pastime in Victorian times – when soup kitchens for the poor were rife – was bowling an iron hoop along the street.)

Box of toys noise
(A late nineteenth-century rhyme probably inspired by the row made when a child delves into a box full of toys.)

Bram Stoker choker
(Irish writer (1847–1912) best known for creating Dracula, who in fairness was more a biter than a choker.)

Brandy butter nutter

Brandy snap slap

Brass band hand

Brass tacks facts
(The phrase 'Getting down to brass tacks' is believed to derive from the practice of nineteenth-century haberdashers who would measure material between brass tacks.)

Bread and butter nutter, gutter

Bread and cheese sneeze

Bread and honey money
('Bread' was first used as slang for 'money' in the 1940s and is also linked to other basic financial expressions, such as 'dough' and 'earning a crust'.)

Bread and jam tram
(A rhyme from the early twentieth century, reflecting the diet of that period.)

Bread and lard hard

Bread knife wife

Brian O'Linn gin
(A phrase so widespread that in the late nineteenth century it was often served in the shorter measure 'Brian'.)

Bricks and mortar daughter

Bride and groom broom, room

Brighton line nine
(The London to Brighton railway was opened in 1841, and in 1843 a third-class ticket from the capital to the coast cost 3s 6d.)

Brixton riot diet
(From the Brixton riots of 1981 which gave the government food for thought.)

Brown Bess yes
('Brown Bess' was the nickname for the British Army's land pattern musket, which was in use from around 1722 to 1838.)

Brown bread dead
(In the 1970s, this replaced 'loaf of bread' as the slang for 'deceased'.)

Bruce Lee key
(After the US-born martial arts actor (1940–73).)

Bruno N'Gotty totty
(French footballer who has played in England for Bolton Wanderers, Birmingham City and Leicester City.)

Brussel sprout Boy Scout, shout

Bryant and Mays stays
(An old type of corset rhymed with the well-known match manufacturers.)

Bubble and squeak beak (magistrate), speak

Bubble gum bum

Buck and doe snow

Bucket afloat coat

Bucket and pail jail
(A rhyme that depicts the act of slopping out. Usually shortened to 'bucket'.)

Bugs Bunny money
(The Warner Bros animated rabbit and lifelong nemesis of Elmer Fudd made his debut in 1939. He was voiced originally by Mel Blanc (1908–89), who famously disliked carrots.)

Bull and cow row (argument)
(Dates back to the nineteenth century and suggests matrimonial discord.)

Bulldozer poser

Bunsen burner nice little earner
(Named after the German chemist Robert Wilhelm Bunsen (1811–99), this phrase could be linked to 'bunce', a common term for money in the nineteenth century.)

Burlington Bertie thirty
('Burlington Bertie from Bow' was a popular music-hall song written in 1915 by William Hargreaves and often sung by his wife, Ella Shields, while dressed as a man.)

Burnt cinder window

Bushel and peck neck
(A bushel and a peck were old units of measurement, a bushel being eight imperial gallons and a peck equalling approximately nine litres.)

Butcher's hook look
(After the double-ended hook used by butchers for hanging up sides of meat and usually shortened to 'butcher's'.)

Buttered bun one

Buttons and bows toes
(From the 1947 Dinah Shore song 'Buttons And Bows', where, too, the title rhymed with 'toes'.)

C

Cab rank bank

Cain and Abel table
(After the biblical sons of Adam and Eve.)

Callard & Bowsers trousers
(English confectionery company founded in 1837 and famous for its butterscotch. Usually shortened to 'Callards' in rhyming slang.)

Camden Town brown (halfpenny)
(In the nineteenth century copper coins were known as 'browns' and in the 1850s the humble halfpenny was rhymed with the north London district of Camden Town.)

Can of Coke joke

Canal boat Tote

Canterbury Tales Wales
(After the collection of stories written by Geoffrey Chaucer in the fourteenth century.)

Captain Bligh pie
(From William Bligh, British naval officer and captain of HMS *Bounty*, whose crew mutinied in 1789.)

Captain Cook look
(Captain James Cook (1728–79) was the Yorkshire-born explorer who claimed the east coast of Australia for Britain.)

Captain Hook book
(The villain of J.M. Barrie's *Peter Pan*.)

Captain Kirk Turk, work
(The captain of the starship *Enterprise* boldly entered the realms of rhyming slang in the 1990s.)

Captain Morgan organ (musical)
(Henry Morgan (1635–88) was a daring Welsh pirate.)

Captain's log bog (toilet)

Car park nark (police informant)

Cardboard box pox

Carl Rosa poser
(Carl Rosa (1842–89) founded an English opera company.
He was a bit grand, which could have led to him being
considered a poser in some circles.)

Carlo Gatti batty
(Swiss entrepreneur Carlo Gatti (1817–78) was supposedly the
first man to make ice cream available to the general public.)

Carving knife wife

Cash and carried married

Cat and mouse house

Cats and mice dice

Centre-half scarf

Chain and locket pocket

Chairman Mao cow
(In vogue from 1966 when *Quotations From Chairman Mao
Tse-Tung* – otherwise known as *The Little Red Book* – was
published. It went on to sell 900 million copies worldwide.)

Chalk Farm arm
(The area of north London located on the Edgware arm of
the Northern Line.)

Charles James Fox box (at the theatre)
(A theatre box has long been known as a 'Charles James' in
memory of Charles James Fox (1749–1806), Whig politician
and Britain's first foreign secretary.)

Charlie Brown clown
(From the 1959 song 'Charlie Brown' by Jerry Leiber and
Mike Stoller, which features the line, 'He's a clown, that
Charlie Brown.' So nothing to do with *Peanuts*.)

Charlie Chan tan
(Charlie Chan appeared in over 40 films in the 1930s and
1940s (played in turn by Warner Oland, Sidney Toler and
Roland Winters).)

Charlie Drakes brakes (on a vehicle)
(Born Charles Springall, diminutive British comedian
Charlie Drake (1925–2006) was famous for his slapstick
routines and 'Hallo, my darlings' catchphrase.)

Charlie Mason basin
(A late nineteenth-century rhyme, usually denoting an
excessive amount rather than a porcelain container. 'He's
had a Charlie Mason' meant 'He's had a basinful'.)

Charlie Prescott waistcoat
(Like Charlie Mason, nobody knows who Charlie Prescott
was but it was a name that rhymed with 'wescot', as 'waistcoat'
used to be pronounced.)

Charlie Pride ride
(A fictional character, not to be confused with US country
music singer Charley Pride.)

Charlie Smirke berk
(Charlie Smirke (1906–93) was a British jockey who won
eleven classics, including four Epsom Derbies.)

Charlton Athletic pathetic
(A rhyme no doubt devised by a Crystal Palace or Millwall
fan.)

Charm and flattery battery

Chas and Dave shave
(Chas Hodges and Dave Peacock turned Cockney pub

culture into a string of hits in the early 1980s, including 'Rabbit', the title of which comes from 'rabbit and pork'.)

Cheddar cheese keys

Cheese grater waiter

Cheesy Quaver favour, raver
(Quavers are a potato snack introduced by Walkers in the 1970s.)

Cheltenham Gold cold
(After steeplechasing's Cheltenham Gold Cup, first run in 1924.)

Cherry hogs dogs (greyhound racing)
(As in, 'I'm just going off to Walthamstow cherries'. A 'cherry hog' is an old term for a cherry stone.)

Cherry pie lie

Cherry ripe pipe
(From the nineteenth century, when cherrywood pipes were popular.)

Chevy Chase face
(After the American entertainer Cornelius ('Chevy') Crane Chase.)

Chew the fat chat
(The first known use of the phrase 'chew the fat' occurred in the 1885 book *Life in the Ranks of the British Army in India* by J. Brunlees Patterson.)

Chicken dinner winner

Chicken oriental mental

Chicken's neck cheque

Chimney and soot foot

China plate mate
(As in, 'Good to see you, me old china.' First recorded in the 1880s, it acquired extensive use during the First World War.)

Chip butty nutty

Chips and peas knees

Chitty Chitty Bang Bang Cockney rhyming slang
(Cockney rhyming slang even has a rhyme of its own in the form of the title of the 1964 children's book written by James Bond creator Ian Fleming.)

Chocolate éclair prayer

Chocolate fudge judge

Christmas cheer beer

Clickety click sixty-six
(First used during the First World War when housie-housie, a forerunner of bingo, was played by the troops.)

Clodhopper copper (police officer)
(This term comes from the oversize boots associated with police officers.)

Clothes pegs legs

Coalman's sack black

Coals and coke broke (penniless)

Coat and badge cadge
(Doggett's Coat and Badge is the prize awarded to the winner of an annual rowing contest for apprentice Thames watermen held between London Bridge and Chelsea.)

Coat hanger clanger

Cockaleekie cheeky
(A traditional Scottish soup derived from the custom whereby the losing bird in a cockfight was plucked, dismembered, and tossed into a pot with several leeks.)

Cock and hen ten

Cock sparrow barrow

Cocoa say so
(As in, 'I should cocoa!')

Coldstream Guards cards (playing)

Collar and tie lie (untruth)

Colonel Blimp shrimp
(A cartoon character devised by David Low for the *Evening Standard* in the 1930s, Colonel Blimp was the ultimate pompous, jingoistic Englishman.)

Colonel Gaddafi café
(The former leader of Libya was more accustomed to a Tripoli palace than a greasy spoon off the Balls Pond Road.)

Comedy Dave rave
('Comedy Dave' is the broadcasting name of David Vitty, who was the sidekick to Radio 1 DJ Chris Moyles from 1998 to 2012.)

Conan Doyle boil (spot)
(After Sir Arthur Conan Doyle (1859–1930), creator of Sherlock Holmes.)

Conger eel squeal (inform on)
(As in, 'If I ever find out who congered on me, he's brown bread'.)

Constant screamer concertina
(Echoing the painful sound that a concertina can make in the wrong hands.)

Cooking fat cat
(A spoonerism as well as rhyming slang.)

Corn on the cob job

Corned beef chief

Corns and bunions onions

Cotton wool pull (chat up)

Cough and choke smoke

Council houses trousers

Country cousin dozen

Couple of bob job
(The implication being that if you got a job, you'd earn some money – from the days when 'bob' was slang for 'shilling'.)

Cow and calf half (pint of beer)

Cream cookie bookie

Cream crackered knackered
('Knackered' derives from the knacker's yards of the mid-nineteenth century where old, worn-out horses were bought and slaughtered for their meat or hide.)

Cribbage pegs legs

Crown Jewels tools

Crust of bread head

Currant bun son, sun, *Sun* newspaper
(When the *Sun*'s owners, News International, launched free internet access via its website in 1999, they traded on the rhyming slang by calling it CurrantBun.com.)

Custard and jelly telly

Custard creams dreams

Cuts and scratches matches
(In the nineteenth century, poor-quality imported safety matches often cut and scratched the side of the box without igniting.)

Cutty Sark loan shark
(Built in 1869, the clipper *Cutty Sark* stands in dry dock at

Greenwich, where it is a familiar London landmark despite being badly damaged by fire in 2007.)

Cynthia Payne stain
(Cynthia Payne hit the headlines in 1978 when she was jailed for eighteen months for running a Streatham brothel, which became known as the 'House of Cyn'.)

D

Dad's Army barmy
(Possibly inspired by the fact that in the Home Guard sitcom *Dad's Army* (1968–77) Captain Mainwaring repeatedly referred to Private Pike as a 'stupid boy'.)

Daffadown dilly silly
(A daffadown dilly was a sixteenth-century name for a daffodil.)

Daft and barmy army

Daily bread head (of family)
(A phrase that became popular in the days when the head of the family was usually the breadwinner.)

Daily Mail ale, tale

Daisy roots boots
(In the 1960 hit 'My Old Man's A Dustman', Lonnie Donegan sang: 'He looks a proper 'nana in his great big hobnail boots/He's got such a job to pull 'em up that he calls 'em daisy roots.')

Dan Dares flares (trousers)
(Created by Frank Hampson for the *Eagle* comic in 1950, Dan Dare was the ultimate space hero.)

Dancing bears stairs

Dancing fleas keys

Darby Kelly (Kel) belly
(As in the line from Harry Champion's song Boiled Beef And Carrots: 'That's the stuff for your Darby Kel, makes you fat and keeps you well'. (See also **Boiled beef and carrot**.))

Date and plum bum

David Jason mason
(English comedy actor who hit the big time in the 1980s as Del Boy Trotter in the BBC's *Only Fools and Horses*.)

Davy Crockett pocket
(The King of the Wild Frontier (1786–1836) serves as a macho alternative to Lucy Locket.)

Day and night light (ale)

Dead loss boss

Deep fat fryer liar

Deep in debt bet
(What you will be if you put too much on the wrong horse.)

Deep sea diver fiver

Desmond (Tutu) 2:2 (degree result)
(The South African clergyman and political activist came to prominence in the 1980s as an opponent of apartheid.)

Desperate Dans cans (headphones)
(The cowboy from Cactusville has been the mainstay of the *Dandy* comic since 1937.)

Diamond rocks socks

Diana Dors drawers (knickers)
(Britain's blonde bombshell of the 1950s, actress Diana Dors (1931–84) was an obvious choice to represent knickers.)

Dick Van Dyke bike
(After the US actor forever remembered for putting on an awful Cockney accent as Bert the chimney sweep in the 1964 film *Mary Poppins*.)

Dickory dock clock
(A term taken from the nursery rhyme 'Hickory Dickory Dock', first published in 1744.)

Dicky bird word
(A familiar rhyming slang phrase, dating back to at least the 1930s.)

Dicky dirt shirt
(A 'dickey' was used to describe an old shirt as far back as 1781.)

Didgeridoo clue
(A didgeridoo is a wind instrument developed by Indigenous Australians.)

Didn't ought port (wine)

Didn't oughta water

Ding dong song

Ding dong bell hell
(From the sixteenth-century nursery rhyme that saw pussy suffer a hellish time in the well until being pulled out by little Tommy Stout.)

Dinner plate mate

Dirty faces laces

Dixie Deans jeans
('Dixie' was the nickname of footballer William Ralph Dean (1907–80) who acquired legendary status by scoring a record 60 League goals for Everton in one season, 1927–28.)

Do me goods Woods (Woodbines)
(Woodbines were a brand of cheap cigarettes popular during the First World War, when it was claimed that cigarettes were healthy.)

Doctor and nurse purse

Dog and bone phone
(First recorded in 1961, as in, 'Get on the dog and order us a Ruby'.)

Dog and pup cup

Dog's meat feet

Dolly Varden garden
(Dolly Varden was a character in *Barnaby Rudge* by Charles Dickens, thus setting the rhyme in the mid-nineteenth century. (See also **Barnaby Rudge**.))

Doner kebab stab

Donkey's ears years
(The 'donkey's ears' rhyme was first recorded in 1916 but made way for the more familiar 'donkey's years' – meaning 'a long time' – in the 1920s.)

Don't make a fuss bus

Doorknob bob (shilling)

Doris Day gay (homosexual)
(From the US singer and actress who was popular in the 1950s and became a gay icon.)

Dot and dash moustache

Doublet and hose nose

Doublet and hosed closed

Douglas Hurd third (degree result)
(The former Conservative politician has been given a raw deal in being associated with a degree that nobody wants.)

Dover boat coat

Dover harbour barber

Down the drain brain

Down the hatch match

(The drinking phrase 'down the hatch' was first recorded in 1931 and its celebratory nature mirrors the euphoria felt when your football team has won its match.)

Drum and fife knife, wife
(A fife is a small flute used in conjunction with a drum in military music.)

Drum roll hole

Dublin trick brick
(Arising from the Irish association with labourers.)

Duchess of Fife wife
(Usually abbreviated to 'Dutch' and immortalised in Albert Chevalier's affectionate 1893 song 'My Old Dutch'.)

Duck and dive jive

Dudley Moores sores
(After the English actor, comedian and musician (1935–2002).)

Duke of York chalk, fork, talk, walk

Dunlop tyre liar

Dustbin lid kid (child)

E

Earls Court salt

Early hours flowers

Earwig twig

East and west chest, vest

East India Docks pox
(After London's Thames-side docks that were built in 1806 and closed in 1967.)

Easter bunny money

Eau de Cologne phone

Edward Heath teeth
(After the former Conservative Prime Minister (1916–2005).)

Egg yolk joke

Eiffel Tower shower

Elephant's trunk drunk

Eliot Ness mess
(A US federal agent based in Chicago, Eliot Ness (1903–57) was responsible for the downfall of mobster Al Capone.)

Engelbert Humperdinck drink
(Named after the sixties crooner born Arnold Dorsey.)

Enoch Powell towel
(From the controversial Conservative MP (1912–98), the towel perhaps being useful for wiping up the 'rivers of blood' that he predicted in his 1968 speech about immigration.)

Errol Flynn chin
(In memory of the swashbuckling, extrovert Australian movie star (1909–59), who took everything on the chin.)

Everton toffee coffee
(Everton toffee was first made in the suburb of Liverpool in the mid-eighteenth century.)

F

Fag packet jacket

False alarm arm

Fanny Cradock haddock
(Cook Fanny Cradock (1909–94) was a television mainstay of the fifties and sixties.)

Fat and wide bride
(The school playground lyrics to Wagner's 'Bridal Chorus' from the opera *Lohengrin* often contain the line, 'Here comes the bride – short, fat and wide'.)

Field of wheat street

Fillet of plaice face

Fine and dandy brandy

Finger and thumb mum, rum

Fireman's hose nose

First-aid blade (knife)
(A dark rhyme, the former suggesting the results of an attack with the latter.)

Fish and tank bank

Fish hook book

Fisherman's daughter water

Five to twos shoes
(Possibly derived from the angle of a person's feet while standing.)

Fleas and ants pants

Flounder and dab cab

Flowery dell cell (prison)
(An ironic rhyme dating back to the 1920s and usually shortened to 'flowery'.)

Fly-by-nights tights

Fly tipper nipper (child)

Fore and aft daft

Forsyte Saga lager
(Inspired by the 1967 BBC adaptation of John Galsworthy's

novel, the show proved so popular that pubs in Britain were deserted on Sunday nights during its 26-week run.)

Fortnum & Mason basin
(After the up-market Piccadilly department store founded in 1707 and renowned for its luxury food hampers.)

Frankie Fraser razor
(After London underworld figure 'Mad' Frankie Fraser who was not averse to using a razor on his victims.)

Frankie Howerd coward
(After comedian Frankie Howerd (1917–92).)

Fred Astaire hair
(Based on the immaculately groomed US actor and dancer (1899–1987) whose real name was Frederick Austerlitz.)

Fridge freezer geezer

Frog and toad road
(First recorded in the 1850s, usually shortened to 'frog'.)

Frog in the throat boat

Fruit and nuts guts

Fruit Gum chum
(Almost certainly stemming from the 1950s TV commercials for Rowntree's Fruit Gums where a small boy pleaded, 'Don't forget the Fruit Gums, Chum'.)

Frying pan old man (husband or father)

Funny feeling ceiling

G

Game of nap cap
(Nap – short for Napoleon – was a popular card game around the turn of the twentieth century.)

Garden fence dense
(No doubt arising from the phrase 'thick as two short planks'.)

Garden gate magistrate, eight

Garden gnome comb

Garden plant aunt

Garden tool fool

Gates of Rome home

Gay Gordon traffic warden
(Based on the nineteenth-century Scottish country dance called the Gay Gordons.)

Geoff Hurst first (degree result), thirst
(It is only proper that England's hat-trick hero of the 1966 World Cup final should be associated with excellence.)

Geoffrey Chaucer saucer
(After the English poet (1340–1400), author of *The Canterbury Tales*.)

George and Ringo bingo
(After George Harrison and Ringo Starr of Beatles fame.)

George Bernard Shaw door
(From the name of the Irish playwright (1856–1950), as in the Larry Grayson catchphrase, 'Shut that George Bernard!')

George Blake snake
(An appropriate rhyme for Englishman George Blake (1922–94), who in 1961 was exposed as a double agent and convicted of spying for the Soviet Union.)

George Melly belly
(Named after the ample stomach of the jazzman, broadcaster and general *bon viveur* (1926–2007).)

George Raft draught
(From the American tough-guy movie star (1895–1980), as in, 'Can you feel the George Raft in here?')

German band hand
('German band' was the name given to groups of strolling musicians that used to play in the streets of London and other major cities in the early twentieth century.)

Gerry Cottle bottle
(Named after the aspiring juggler who ran away to join the circus at the age of fifteen in 1961 and was running his own circus within ten years.)

Gert and Daisy lazy
(Popular Cockney characters from 1930s and 1940s radio created by comedy double act Elsie (1895–1990) and Doris (1904–78) Waters.)

Gertie Gitana banana
(Gertie Gitana (1888–1957) was a music-hall singer from the early twentieth century.)

Gilbey's gin chin
(The name 'Gilbey's' has been seen on bottles of gin since 1872, its London dry gin being a particular favourite.)

Ginger ale jail

Giraffe laugh
(As in, 'Is he having a giraffe?')

Girl and boy toy

Girls and boys noise

Give and take cake

Glasgow Ranger stranger

Glass of beer ear

Glass of plonk conk (nose)

Glenn Hoddle doddle
(From the gifted footballer who found his short reign as England manager anything but a doddle.)

God almighty nightie

God forbid kid (child)
(From the early twentieth century and apparently inspired by the lament of an impoverished man at the prospect of yet another mouth to feed.)

Gold watch Scotch (whisky)
(This nineteenth-century rhyme surely stems from the colour of whisky.)

Golden Hind blind
(After the name of the ship in which Sir Francis Drake sailed around the world between 1577 and 1580.)

Goldilocks pox

Gone to bed dead

Goodie and baddie paddy (Irishman)

Goose's neck cheque

Gooseberry puddin' woman
(A twentieth-century term whereby a man might refer to his wife as his 'old gooseberry'.)

Granny's wrinkles winkles

Grape vine clothes line

Grass in the park nark (police informant)
(A rhyme that uses the 1930s term 'grass' for 'informant' (probably from 'snake in the grass') to link up with 'nark', which dates back to the mid-nineteenth century.)

Grasshopper copper (police officer)

Greengages wages
(First recorded in 1931 and often shortened to 'greens', a colour associated with money not least because pound notes were green.)

Greens and brussels muscles
(A rhyme originating from the belief that eating your greens helps build up muscles.)

Grey mare fare
(Originating from the days of nineteenth-century horse-drawn transport.)

Grumble and mutter flutter (bet)

Guinea pig wig

Haddock and bloater motor

Hail and rain train

Hairy knees please

Hale and hearty party

Half a crown brown (snooker ball)
(A half-crown was worth two shillings and sixpence (12½p) until the coin was discontinued in 1967.)

Half a nicker vicar
(In Cockney slang a 'nicker' was £1, so in old money 'half a nicker' was ten shillings (or 50p in today's terms).)

Half and half scarf

Half-inch pinch (steal)
(First recorded in 1925, as in, 'Who's half-inched me half and half?')

Half-ounce bounce (a cheque)
(The common factor in this rhyme is a short measure.)

Half-ouncer bouncer (doorman)

Halfpenny dip ship
(A London dockers' rhyme from the mid-nineteenth century, referring to a halfpenny lucky dip in a sweet shop.)

Halfpenny stamp tramp

Ham and cheesy easy

Ham shanks Yanks (Americans)

Hammer and discus whiskers

Hampstead Heath teeth
(Usually shortened to 'Hampsteads', this term was first recorded in 1887.)

Hands and feet meat

Hanger Lane pain
(Meaning a 'pain in the neck', which the infamous Hanger Lane gyratory system, introduced in the 1970s, certainly is. In 2007 it was named Britain's scariest road junction.)

Hank Marvin starvin'
(After the Shadows' guitarist Hank Marvin (born Brian Robson Rankin).)

Hansel and Gretel kettle
(The two young heroes of the Brothers Grimm fairy tale cooked the wicked witch in her own oven.)

Harbour light right

Hard labour neighbour

Hare and hound round (of drinks)

Harold Macmillan villain
(The Conservative politician (1894–1986) who, as Prime

Minister, sacked seven members of his cabinet during the 'Night of the Long Knives' in July 1962.)

Harold Pinter splinter
(From the renowned English playwright.)

Harry Lime time
(Harry Lime was the enigmatic central character in Graham Greene's 1950 novel *The Third Man*. In the film version Lime was played by Orson Welles.)

Harvey Nichols pickles
(In honour of the upmarket department store founded in 1813 by Benjamin Harvey as a linen shop in London's Knightsbridge.)

Has beens greens (vegetables)

Hat and coat boat

Hat and feather weather

Hat and scarf bath

Hattie Jacques the shakes
(Comedy actress (1922–80) best known for playing Eric Sykes's sister in his long-running TV series and for appearing in fourteen *Carry On* films.)

Heap of coke bloke
(From the days when London homes had coal fires, sometimes shortened to 'heapy'.)

Heaven and hell smell

Heavenly bliss kiss

Hedge and ditch pitch

Henry Fonda Honda
(The US actor (1905–82) gave his name to the Honda 90 motorbike on which many aspiring taxi drivers toured the streets of London learning 'The Knowledge'.)

Herbie Hides strides (trousers)
(British boxer Herbie Hide was twice WBO heavyweight champion in the 1990s. 'Strides' has been a colloquialism for 'trousers' since the start of the twentieth century.)

Here and there chair

Herring and kipper stripper

Hey diddle diddle fiddle
(Inspired by the eighteenth-century nursery rhyme and the increasing use of the word 'diddle' to mean 'cheat'.)

Hide and seek cheek (nerve)

Highland fling ring, king (in playing cards)

Hit and miss kiss
(Popular from the early 1960s, possibly inspired by the 'hit' or 'miss' cards held up by panellists on BBC television's *Juke Box Jury*.)

Hokey-cokey karaoke
(The hokey-cokey is a song and dance that originated in England during the early 1940s. Karaoke – meaning 'empty orchestra' – started in Japan in the 1970s.)

Holy Ghost post (mail), toast

Honey bees keys

Horn of Plenty twenty
(In Greek mythology the Horn of Plenty was the name given to a goat's horn filled with fruit and an abundance of other appetising foodstuffs.)

Horse and carriage garage

Horse and trough cough
(Usually shortened to 'horse', whose similarity to 'hoarse' makes it suitable for a throaty rhyme.)

Horses and carts darts

Hot beef stop thief
(The word 'beef' has been used as a rhyme for 'thief' since at least the 1740s and in the nineteenth century 'hot beef' became the accepted Cockney cry aimed at a fleeing felon.)

Hot cross bun nun
(The cross on the bun is a symbol of the crucifixion (they are traditionally eaten on Good Friday).)

Hot dinner winner

Hot potato waiter
(A rhyme aided by the Cockney pronunciation 'potater'.)

House of Lords cords (corduroy trousers)

Housemaid's knee sea

How's your father? lather (state)
(As in, 'Just because I was a few minutes late he was in a right how's your father'.)

Huckleberry Hound pound
(Created by Hanna-Barbera and voiced by Daws Butler, Huckleberry Hound had his own TV cartoon show from 1958, supported by Yogi Bear and Pixie and Dixie.)

Hugs and kisses missus (wife)

Hundred to thirty dirty
(From horse-race betting odds, a shade over three to one.)

Hurricane lamp tramp

I

I suppose nose
(First recorded in the 1850s, as in, 'What's that hanging from his I suppose?')

In and out gout

In the mood food

Incredible Hulk sulk
(Created by Stan Lee and Jack Kirby for *Marvel Comics* in 1962, Dr Bruce Banner is a scientist who, whenever he gets really angry, is transformed into the Incredible Hulk.)

Inky blue flu

Inky smudge judge

Irish jig wig
(First used in the 1970s and generally shortened to 'Irish'.)

Irish stew true

Iron girder murder

Iron tank bank

Isle of Wight right

Itchy teeth beef

Ivory pearl girl
(As in, 'Diamonds are an ivory's best friend'.)

J

Jabba the Hutt shut
(In honour of the obese, slug-like creature from *Star Wars*.)

Jack and Dandy handy

Jack and Jill hill

Jack in the box pox

Jack Jones on your own
(This rhyme originated during the First World War, as in, 'Now his hugs and kisses has left him, he's all on his Jack Jones.')

Jack Ketch stretch
(Jack Ketch was an English executioner of the seventeenth century, whose attention was therefore even less welcome to a convicted felon than a prison sentence or 'stretch'.)

Jack of Spades shades (sunglasses)

Jack Sprat brat, fat
(Named after the world's most incompatible eaters – 'Jack Sprat could eat no fat, his wife could eat no lean'.)

Jack tar bar
(A 'jack tar' is an old name for a sailor – derived from the tar with which sailors used to waterproof their trousers in the eighteenth century.)

Jack the Lad bad
(The original Jack the Lad was an eighteenth-century thief called Jack Sheppard.)

Jack the Ripper kipper
(The way in which a herring is sliced open is eerily reminiscent of the manner in which the 1888 Whitechapel serial killer slit open his victims.)

Jack the Rippers slippers

Jackanory story
(In rhyming slang 'jackanory' refers to a tall story (basically a lie) rather than the sort of tale read by Bernard Cribbins and co. on the BBC children's series *Jackanory* (1965–96).)

Jacket and vest West (End of London)
(As in, 'He must have something up his sleeve because he's going up the jacket this afternoon'.)

Jackie Chan plan
(After the Chinese martial arts actor.)

Jam roll parole, the dole

Jam tart heart

Jamaica rum thumb

James Dean keen
(US actor (1931–55) whose premature death in a car crash proved a shrewd career move.)

James Hunt front (nerve)
(From the courageous and outspoken British racing driver (1947–93), as in, 'You ain't 'alf got some James Hunt!')

Jamjar car
(Originating in the 1930s, the term has achieved such widespread acceptance that the UK's biggest online new car dealer is called jamjar.com.)

Jean Michel Jarre bar
(The first two-thirds of the French composer's name are also used to refer to a 'jar' (a pint glass) of beer. So you could order a Jean Michel while standing at the Jean Michel.)

Jeff Beck cheque
(A 1970s rhyme based on the influential English rock guitarist, formerly with The Yardbirds.)

Jeffrey Dahmer charmer
(A rhyme laden with irony to describe the cannibalistic US serial killer (1960–94) who was anything but a charmer.)

Jekyll and Hydes strides (trousers)
(From Robert Louis Stevenson's character with the split personality, usually shortened in rhyming slang to 'jekylls'.)

Jellied eel deal

Jellied eels wheels (transport)
(As in, 'How are you getting home? Have you got jellied eels?')

Jelly bone phone

Jelly tot spot

Jet fighter all nighter

Jimi Hendrix appendix
(From the US rock guitarist (1942–70).)

Jimmy Cliff whiff
(Based on the Jamaican reggae singer who enjoyed UK chart success in the late 1960s and early 1970s.)

Jimmy Connors honours
(As in, 'Will you do the Jimmy Connors, mate?')

Jimmy Greaves thieves
(As the outstanding goal poacher of his generation, footballer Jimmy Greaves scored over 350 goals between 1957 and 1971.)

Jimmy Hill chill
(After the veteran footballer and broadcaster, as in, 'There's a bit of a Jimmy Hill in the air today.')

Jimmy Logie bogey
('Snot much fun for the Arsenal footballer (1919–84) being rhymed with nasal mucus.)

Jimmy Riddle piddle
(First recorded in the 1930s and has become a universal byword for bladder-emptying. Sometimes shortened to just 'Jimmy', as in, 'Get 'em in while I go for a quick Jimmy.')

Joan of Arc lark
(The name of the saint and French heroine (c.1412–31) is mainly evoked in a sense of exasperation, as in, 'Blow this for a Joan of Arc!')

Joanna piano
(First recorded in 1846 and still going strong, 'joanna' is very much a Cockney knees-up piano.)

Jockey's whip kip (sleep)

Jockeys' whips chips

Joe Baksi taxi
(A US heavyweight boxer (1922–77), Baksi's name was frequently used as rhyming slang in Irvine Welsh's book *Trainspotting*.)

Joe Blake steak

Joe O'Gorman foreman

John Bull on the pull
(A symbol of British nationalism, John Bull was created by Dr John Arbuthnot in 1712.)

John Cleese cheese
(The comedy actor's family name was actually Cheese until his father changed it in 1915.)

John O'Groats oats
(As in, 'Look at the smile on his face – you can tell he's been getting his John O'Groats lately.')

John Wayne train
(The US Western actor (1907–79) was more familiar with a wagon train than the 8.25 from Dartford to Charing Cross.)

John West very best
(From the fish producer whose TV adverts proclaimed that only the best was good enough for John West.)

Johnnie Walker talker
(The rhyme is based on the brand of whisky, dating from the nineteenth century, the implication being that too much of it loosens your tongue.)

Johnny Horner corner
(Dating from the late nineteenth century when pubs were invariably situated on street corners, so 'going round the Johnny' meant going for a pint.)

Jolly joker poker

Jolly Roger lodger
(Taken from the popular term for a pirate's flag that was first coined in the early eighteenth century and emphasising the commonly held view that lodgers weren't to be trusted.)

Judge Dredd head
(The law enforcer who first featured in the sci-fi comic *2000 AD* in 1977.)

Julius Caesar geezer
(The distinguished Roman statesman (100–44 BC) might not have been too impressed had Brutus and Cassius referred to him as a 'geezer'.)

K

Kate and Sidney steak and kidney
(A partial spoonerism dating from the early twentieth century.)

Keith Moon loon
(Keith Moon (1947–78) was the wildman drummer of The Who, his erratic behaviour earning the nickname 'Moon the loon'.)

Ken Dodd wad
(When the Liverpudlian comedian was charged with tax evasion in 1989, it was revealed that he kept a sizeable wad of money stashed in suitcases in his attic.)

Kermit the frog bog (toilet)

Kettle and hob fob (watch)

Kick and prance dance

Kidney punch lunch

King Canutes boots
(An early twentieth-century rhyme based on the Danish king of England (reign 1016–35).)

King dick thick (stupid)

King Lears ears

Kingdom come bum

Kings and queens baked beans

Kipper and bloater photo

Kipper and plaice face
(Another rhyme exploiting the common insult 'fish face'.)

Kiss and cuddle muddle

Kitchen sink clink (jail), drink

Kitty litter bitter (beer)

Knobbly knees keys
(In the 1950s many Londoners spent their summer break at the coast. While the girls took part in beauty contests, the male equivalent was the knobbly knees contest.)

Knock at the door four

Knocker and knob job
(Possibly inspired by the old practice of going from door to door in search of work.)

Kuala Lumpur jumper
(A rhyme based on the capital of Malaysia.)

Kung fu fighter cigarette lighter

L

La-di-da cigar
(First recorded in 1977, a clear reference to the perceived superior social standing of cigar smokers.)

Lady Godiva fiver
(According to legend, Lady Godiva, the wife of Leofric, Earl of Mercia, rode naked through the streets of Coventry in the eleventh century to persuade her husband to lower taxes.)

Lady in silk milk

Lager and lime time

Lager lout kraut (German)
(A 1990s insult for the nation that brews arguably the best lager in the world.)

Lambeth Walk chalk
(Written by Douglas Furber and Noel Gay, 'The Lambeth Walk' was a song-and-dance number from the 1937 musical *Me and My Girl*.)

Larry Grayson Mason
(From the camp comic (1923–95) whose catchphrase 'Shut that door' and unseen friend Everard helped propel him to national prominence in the 1970s.)

Last card of the pack the sack
(A rhyme inspired by the expression 'getting your cards', meaning 'to get the sack'.)

Laugh and joke smoke (cigarette)
(A rhyme that was popular in the first half of the twentieth century when men and women would gather for a laugh and joke while enjoying a smoke.)

Laugh and titter bitter (beer)

Left and right fight
(A neat rhyme conjuring up images of blows in a boxing match.)

Left in the lurch church
(A nineteenth-century phrase that must have been particularly poignant for any bride left waiting at the altar.)

Leg of beef thief

Lemon and lime crime

Lemon drop cop (police officer)

Lemon squeezer geezer

Lemon squeezy easy
(As in the familiar children's rhyme 'easy peasy lemon squeezy'.)

Lemon tart smart

Len Hutton button
(From the Yorkshire and England batsman (1916–90) who captained his country in the 1950s.)

Lester Piggott bigot
(Famously monosyllabic British jockey who rode over 5,000 winners, including nine Epsom Derbies, and served a jail sentence in 1987 for tax evasion.)

Life and death breath

Lilley and Skinner beginner
(After the British shoe manufacturers founded in 1835.)

Lillian Gish fish
(Hollywood actress (1893–1993) who began her career in 'the silents' and made her final film in 1987 at the age of 93.)

Limehouse Cut gut (paunch)
(The oldest canal in London, the Limehouse Cut provides a

short cut from the Thames at Limehouse Basin to the River Lee Navigation.)

Linen draper newspaper
(Dating from the nineteenth century and usually shortened to 'linen'.)

Lion's lair chair
(This twentieth-century rhyme is based on the notion that the head of the house has his favourite chair and that it is unwise – dangerous even – for anyone else to attempt to sit in it.)

Lion's roar snore

Lionel Blair chair

Lionel Blairs flares (trousers)
(After the happy hoofer who carried off the seventies fashions with more style than most.)

Little brown jug plug
(Derived from the 1869 song 'Little Brown Jug' by Joseph Winner that was popularised 70 years later by Glenn Miller.)

Little Nell bell
(From the tragic character in Charles Dickens's *Old Curiosity Shop*. The term is usually applied to a doorbell, as in, 'Who's that ringing on the Little Nell at this hour?')

Little Red Riding Hoods stolen goods
(From the Brothers Grimm fairytale.)

Little Tich itch
(Little Tich was the stage name of 4ft 6in music-hall comedian Harry Relph (1867–1928) whose most celebrated routine was his Big Boot Dance.)

Loaf of bread head
(Always shortened to 'loaf', as in the familiar expression 'use your loaf' (meaning 'be sensible'), which first appeared in print in 1938.)

Lollipop shop
(This can be used in the sense of 'to inform on' as well as to denote a retail outlet.)

London Bridge fridge
(A bridge has existed at or near the present site for nearly 2,000 years. The current London Bridge – at least the seventh – was opened in 1973.)

London fog dog
(When householders burned coal fires, dense fogs – or pea soupers or smogs as they became known – hung ominously over London for days at a time.)

London taxi jacksie (backside)

Long Acre baker
(A rhyme first recorded in the nineteenth century and named after the street near Covent Garden.)

Looby Loos shoes
(After the doll in the 1950s children's TV series *Andy Pandy*, as in, 'Check out the new Loobies'.)

Loop the loop soup

Lord and mastered plastered (drunk)

Lord Lovell shovel
(The rhyme has its origins among nineteenth-century sailors although nobody is sure which of the many Lord Lovells it actually concerns.)

Lord Mayor swear
(Perhaps because the Lord Mayor of London has to swear allegiance to the sovereign.)

Lord of the Manor tanner (sixpence)
(Introduced in 1551, the sixpence – nicknamed a 'tanner' and the equivalent of 2½p – continued in circulation until decimalisation in 1971.)

Lords and peers ears

Lorna Doone spoon
(Inspired by the heroine of Exmoor from the 1869 novel *Lorna Doone* by R. D. Blackmore.)

Lost and found pound

Love and kisses missus

Lucky charm arm

Lucky dip chip, kip (sleep)

Lucy Locket pocket
(From the nineteenth-century nursery rhyme: 'Lucy Locket lost her pocket'.)

Lump of ice advice

Lump of lead head

M

Macaroni pony (£25)
(A 'macaroni' was an eighteenth-century English term for a dandy. The rhyme with 'pony' stems from the song 'Yankee Doodle', a British jibe at US fashions. (See also **Yankee Doodles**.))

Mackerel and sprat prat

Mae West best, chest
(After the American actress (1893–1980) whose chest was so admired by Allied soldiers during the Second World War that they called their inflatable life jackets 'Mae Wests' because the shape reminded them of her generous bosom.)

Magistrate's court short (drink)

(Probably a warning as to where you are likely to end up if you drink too many shorts.)

Mahatma Gandhi brandy
(Named after the Indian nationalist leader and teetotaller (1869–1948).)

Major Stevens evens (betting odds)
(A fictitious character to describe a situation when the odds are one to one or fifty-fifty.)

Man alive five

Man and wife knife

Man on the moon spoon

Manfred Mann plan
(South African-born keyboard player whose band had a string of hits in the 1960s, including 'Do Wah Diddy Diddy' and 'Pretty Flamingo'.)

Mangle and wringer singer
(A mangle and wringer was a common sight in British households before the advent of washing machines in the late 1950s.)

Manhole cover brother
(A partly anatomical expression to rhyme with the Cockney 'bruvver'.)

Marbles and conkers bonkers

Margate sands hands

Marie Corelli telly
(An early rhyme for television taken from the pseudonym of the British romantic novelist Mary Mackay (1855–1924).)

Marquis de Sade hard
(French aristocrat and writer (1740–1814) whose pleasure at inflicting pain on others gave rise to the term 'sadism'.)

Mars bar scar
(Introduced in 1932, the phrase entered Cockney rhyming slang in the 1970s, chiefly to denote the sort of scar received in a gang fight.)

Maud and Ruth truth

Merry-go-round pound
(Suggesting the circulation of currency.)

Merry old soul coal
(From the eighteenth-century nursery rhyme 'Old King Cole', who was a merry old soul.)

Mexican wave shave
(The ultimate sign of spectator boredom at a sporting event first manifested itself at the 1986 Mexico World Cup.)

Michael Caine pain, stain
(The actor's London roots – in his youth he worked as a porter at Smithfield meat market – make him a natural for Cockney rhyming slang.)

Michael Winner dinner
(A simple rhyme for the food critic and *bon viveur*.)

Mickey Duff rough
(The British boxing promoter's battered face is testament to his own pugilistic past.)

Mickey Monk drunk

Mickey Mouse house

Mickey Mouser Scouser
(Since his debut in 1928, the Walt Disney rodent's name has come to be a colloquialism for 'substandard' or 'amateurish'.)

Mickie Most toast
(After the record producer (1938–2003) who brought the world Suzi Quatro and was a regular judge on the 1970s TV talent show *New Faces*.)

Mile End friend
(From the area of East London that gets its name because it is one mile east of the boundary of the City of London.)

Mince pies eyes
(First recorded in 1857 and generally shortened to 'minces'.)

Moan and wail jail

Moby Dick sick
(From the fearsome great white whale in the 1851 novel *Moby Dick* by Herman Melville.)

Mona Lisa pizza
(One Italian work of art representing another even though Leonardo Da Vinci probably never envisaged *La Gioconda* with an anchovy topping.)

Monkey's tail nail

Monty's army barmy
(The troops in question were those commanded by General Montgomery in the Second World War.)

Morecambe and Wise flies
(Eric Morecambe (1926–84) and Ernie Wise (1925–99) were a much-loved comedy double act for 43 years.)

Moriarty party
(It seems unlikely that the Moriarty in question is either Sherlock Holmes's arch enemy, Professor Moriarty, or Spike Milligan's Count Jim Moriarty from *The Goon Show*.)

Mortar and trowel towel

Mother Goose loose
(Thought to be based on Bertha *pied d'oie* (Goose-foot Bertha), wife of King Robert II who ruled France from 996 to 1031.)

Mother Hubbard cupboard
(From the sad tale – first published in 1805 – of Old Mother

Hubbard who went to the cupboard to fetch her poor dog a bone, only to find that the shelves were bare.)

Mother-in-law saw
(No doubt stemming from the fact that one has a sharp tongue and the other has sharp teeth.)

Mother of pearl girl

Mother's pride bride

Mrs Moore floor
(From the character in the 1926 Harry Castling and James Walsh comic song 'Don't Have Any More, Mrs Moore'.)

Mrs Mopp shop
(A 1940s expression taken from the charlady character in the radio comedy *ITMA* – 'It's That Man Again' – a reference to Hitler.)

Muddy trench the bloody French
(A rhyme dug out in the trenches of the First World War.)

Mum and Dad mad

Murray Mint skint
(A line of confectionery that became part of popular culture in the late 1950s thanks to a series of amusing TV commercials.)

Murray Walker talker
(If ever a rhyme suited a celebrity, it is to label the veteran motor racing commentator a 'talker'. Motormouth Murray was never at a loss for words.)

Mustard and cress dress

Muswell Hill bill
(From the district of north London, as in, 'Oi, cheese grater, can I have the Muswell?')

Mutter and stutter butter

Myrna Loy saveloy
(Actress Myrna Loy (1905–93) was voted 'Queen of Hollywood' in 1938.)

N

Nanny goat coat, throat
(Usually abbreviated to 'nanny', as in, 'I've got a frog in my nanny'.)

Nat King Cole the dole
(From the unforgettable American singer (1919–65), as in, 'Are you gonna spend your entire life on the Nat King Cole?')

Needle and pin gin, thin

Needle and thread bread

Needles and pins twins
(As in, 'Congratulations, you've got needles!')

Nell Gwynn gin
(Charles II's mistress (1650–87) was famed for selling oranges, which just happen to go very nicely with gin.)

Nellie Deans greens

Nellie Duff puff (life)
(This rhyme is the origin of the phrase 'not on your nellie', first heard in the 1940s and meaning 'not on your life', since 'puff' is slang for 'life'.)

Nelson Eddys readies (cash)
(From American singer Nelson Eddy (1901–67).)

Nelson Riddle piddle
(A wee honour for the US composer and orchestra leader (1921–85).)

Nervo and Knox goggle box (TV)
(Although mainly at home on the stage, Crazy Gang duo
Jimmy Nervo (1890–1975) and Teddy Knox (1896–1974)
made occasional appearances on the 'goggle box'.)

Nervous wreck cheque
(A rhyme drawing on the emotions felt while waiting for a
large payment to arrive in the post.)

New Delhi belly
(This term is derived from the rush of diarrhoea known
as 'Delhi belly' that sometimes results from eating poorly
prepared Indian food on the sub-continent.)

Newgate Gaol tale
(The tale in question is the type of hard-luck yarn that might
be spun by a prisoner. Newgate jail operated for over 700
years on the site of what is now the Old Bailey.)

Nigel Mansell cancel
(After the 1992 Formula One world champion.)

Night and day grey

Night Boat to Cairo giro
('Night Boat To Cairo' was the title track of the 1979 debut
album by Madness, and 'giro' is a slang term for 'the dole'.)

No surrenders suspenders

Noah's Ark lark, nark (informant), park

Noddy Holders shoulders
(After the singer with 1970s band Slade.)

North and south mouth
(Cockney singer Tommy Steele's 1960 recording 'What a
Mouth' contained the lines: 'What a mouth, what a mouth,
what a north and south, Blimey what a mouth he's got!')

Nose and chin win
(The abbreviated version 'nose' may be the basis of the

expression 'on the nose', a horse-racing term describing a bet laid for a win only rather than each way.)

Nuclear sub pub

Nursery rhymes *The Times*
(A whimsical rhyme linking a children's pursuit with arguably Britain's most grown-up newspaper.)

Obi-Wan Kenobi mobi (mobile phone)
(After the Jedi Master from *Star Wars*.)

Ocean liner shiner (black eye)

Ocean wave shave

Oi Jimmy Knacker tobacco
(Oi Jimmy Knacker was a children's street game similar to leapfrog that was popular in London in the 1920s. The rhyme works because of the Cockney pronunciation 'tabakker'.)

Old fogey bogey (snot)

Old iron and brass grass
(From the rag and bone man's collection call of 'any old iron', popularised by the 1911 music-hall song of that title performed by Harry Champion.)

Old King Cole the dole

Old oak the Smoke (London)
('The Smoke' has been London's nickname from the nineteenth century on account of its polluted atmosphere from homes and factories.)

Omar Sharif grief
(After the smooth Egyptian actor, as in, 'Will you stop giving me so much Omar!')

On and off cough

On the floor poor
(A rhyme reflecting where you might end up sleeping if you've got no money.)

Ones and twos shoes

Ooh la la bra

Orange peel feel

Overcoat maker undertaker
(A 'wooden overcoat' is a slang term for 'coffin'.)

Oxford scholar collar, dollar
(In the mid-nineteenth century there were about four US dollars to the pound and so five shillings became known as a 'dollar', which was converted to an 'Oxford scholar'.)

P

Pain in the neck cheque
(Which it could be if you had to write a large one.)

Pair of kippers slippers

Pall Mall gal (girl)

Panoramas pyjamas
(A rhyme used chiefly by parents to encourage children in the 1950s to go to bed, as in, 'Come on, time to get your panoramas on'.)

Pantomime cow row (argument)

Paper bag nag

Paraffin lamp tramp
(Usually abbreviated to 'paraffin' in recognition of the liquid refreshment associated with down-and-outs.)

Partick Thistle whistle
(After the poor relations of Glasgow football whose lack of success led fan Billy Connolly to remark: 'I grew up thinking they were called Partick Thistle Nil'.)

Pattie Hearst first (degree result)
(The American heiress hit the headlines in 1974 when, after being kidnapped by members of the Symbionese Liberation Army, she helped them rob a San Francisco bank.)

Peace and quiet diet

Peanut butter nutter

Pearly Gate plate

Pea shooter hooter (nose)

Peas in the pot hot

Pebble-dashed smashed (drunk)

Peckham Rye tie
(Dating from the nineteenth century and commemorating the thoroughfare in south-east London.)

Pen and ink stink

Penny-a-mile tile (hat)
(A rhyme popular at the turn of the twentieth century when George Spartels wrote the music-hall song 'Where Did You Get That Hat?', with the line: 'Where did you get that tile?')

Penny Black back
(The Penny Black was the name of the first British postage stamp, issued in 1840.)

Penny locket pocket

Percy Sledge wedge (money)
(US soul singer whose biggest hit was the 1966 classic 'When A Man Loves A Woman'.)

Percy Thrower blower (telephone)
(After the television gardening guru (1913–88), as in, 'Who was that on the Percy Thrower?')

Pete Tong wrong
(After the Radio 1 disc jockey. A 2004 comedy film about a DJ who goes deaf was titled *It's All Gone Pete Tong*.)

Peter O'Toole stool
(This refers mainly to a bar stool, a favourite perch for the notoriously thirsty Irish actor.)

Peter Pan can (safe), van
(Hence the confusing instruction from the leader of a gang of ram-raiders, 'Quick, get the Peter Pan into the Peter Pan!')

Petrol pump hump
(Meaning bad mood, as in, 'You didn't 'arf have the petrol pump last night'.)

Peyton Place face
(Based on the 1956 novel of the same title, *Peyton Place* debuted on British television in 1965 and was the first soap to be imported from the US.)

Phil the Fluter shooter (gun)
('Shooter' has been slang for 'gun' since the nineteenth century and is rhymed with the central character in the traditional Irish ballad 'Phil The Fluter's Ball'.)

Philharmonic gin and tonic

Photo finish Guinness

Piccadilly silly
(After the central London street so named after a local tailor named Robert Baker who specialised in making 'piccadils' – fashionable collars with lace borders.)

Pick and choose booze

Pick up sticks six

Pickled onion bunion

Pie and liquor vicar

Pieces of eight weight
(Usually condensed to 'pieces'.)

Pig in the middle piddle

Pig's ear beer
(From the late nineteenth century and thus predating the
other (non-rhyming) slang use for 'pig's ear' meaning a
'cock-up'.)

Pig's trotter squatter

Pillar and post ghost
(The saying 'from pillar to post' apparently refers to the
pillars and posts that were part of the indoor courts used for
the game of real tennis.)

Pimple and blotch Scotch (whisky)

Pin pegs legs
(Shortened to 'pins'. (See also **Rin Tin Tins**.))

Pinky and Perky turkey
(After the singing puppet pigs. An episode of their show
titled 'You Too Can Be a Prime Minister' was banned by the
BBC in 1966 for fear that it might influence the forthcoming
general election.)

Pirates of Penzance pants
(From the Gilbert and Sullivan comic opera that premiered
in 1879.)

Plates of meat feet
(First appeared in print in 1887 when an edition of *Referee*
included the lines: 'As she walked along the street with her
little plates of meat, And the summer sunshine falling, On
her golden Barnet Fair'.)

Pleasure and pain rain

Plinkety plonk vin blanc (white wine)
(First coined by Australian troops serving in France during the First World War and subsequently reduced to 'plonk'.)

Polly parrots carrots

Polo mint skint
(After the sweet introduced by Rowntree in 1948.)

Poor relation station
(This rhyme originated in the early twentieth century when only the wealthy could afford cars, leaving everyone else to travel by train.)

Pop goes the weasel diesel
(From the seventeenth-century nursery rhyme.)

Pork chop cop
(No doubt inspired by the fact that 'pig' has been a derogatory term for a police officer since at least 1811.)

Pork pies lies
(First recorded in the 1980s but now so well established that it is frequently abbreviated to 'porkies'.)

Porky Pig big
(After the cartoon pig who made his debut for Warner Bros in 1935.)

Pot and pan old man (husband or father)

Pot of glue clue

Potatoes in the mould cold
(Derived from the horticultural practice of covering potatoes still in the ground with a heap of earth to protect them from frost, and now reduced to the more familiar 'taters'.)

Pots and dishes wishes

Pound note coat

Pounds and pence sense

Pride and joy boy

Punch and Judy moody
(The traditional children's entertainment dates back to sixteenth-century Italy and a character called Punchinello who was then anglicised in the UK as Mr Punch in 1662.)

Q

Quaker Oat coat
(After the US porridge-making company formed in 1901 and with a nod to the warmth provided by both a bowl of the cereal and an overcoat.)

Queens Park Ranger stranger
(After the West London football club and first heard in the 1960s.)

Quentin Crisp lisp
(Quentin Crisp (1908–99) became an author, raconteur and gay icon after changing his name from the less exotic Denis Pratt.)

R

Rabbit and pork talk
(Since its inception around 1941, this rhyme has entered mainstream dialect as 'rabbit'.)

Radio Rental mental
(Based on the name of TV rental firm Radio Rentals, this rhyme first appeared in the 1970s.)

Rag and bone throne (toilet)

Raging thirst first (degree result)

Randolph Scott spot
(From the US actor (1903–87), a celluloid Western hero of the 1940s.)

Rant and rave shave

Rasher and bubble double (in darts)
(From the cheap dish of bacon and bubble and squeak, which is leftover mashed potatoes and cabbage. (See also **Bubble and squeak**.))

Raspberry tart fart
(Blowing 'raspberries' to make a farting sound has been a playground pursuit since the nineteenth century.)

Rattle and clank bank

Read and write fight

Reeling and rocking stocking
(A rhyme from the rock 'n' roll era when fashions were becoming more daring; taken from the title of Chuck Berry's 1958 track 'Reelin' And Rockin'.)

Rhubarb crumble grumble

Rhythm and blues shoes

Ribbon and curl girl

Richard Burtons curtains
(After the noted Welsh actor (1925–84).)

Richard Todd cod
(After the British actor, as in, 'I'll have a Richard Todd and a portion of Jaggers, please'.)

Riff raff Taff (Welsh)

Rifle range change (money)

Rinky dink pink (snooker ball)

Rin Tin Tins pins (legs)

(German Shepherd dog Rin Tin Tin – affectionately known as 'Rinty' – was a movie star from the 1920s and a TV star in the 1950s. (See also **Pin pegs**.))

Rip and tear swear

Rip Van Winkle tinkle (pee)
(Created in an 1819 short story by US author Washington Irving.)

Rising damp cramp
(This phrase enjoyed a new lease of life with Eric Chappell's 1970s comedy series starring Leonard Rossiter as seedy landlord Rigsby.)

River Nile denial
(As in, 'He just won't admit it – I'm afraid he's in the River Nile'.)

River Ouse booze

River Tyne wine

Roast beef teeth

Roast pork fork

Rob Roy boy
(In recognition of Scottish outlaw Rob Roy McGregor (1671–1734), sometimes known as the Scottish Robin Hood and hero of Walter Scott's 1818 novel *Rob Roy*.)

Roberta Flack sack
(The name of the American singer not only signifies job dismissal but also the colloquial meaning of 'sack' as 'bed'.)

Robin Hood good
(Mainly used in a negative manner, as in, 'What did you buy that for? That's no Robin Hood!')

Robinson and Cleaver fever
(After a draper's store that opened in London's Regent Street at the end of the nineteenth century.)

Rock 'n' roll dole

Rock of ages wages
(Based on the title of the popular hymn written by Revd Augustus Montague Toplady and first published in 1775.)

Rocking horse sauce

Rocks and boulders shoulders

Rogan Josh dosh (money)
(A 1990s rhyme cooked up by lovers of the aromatic curry dish.)

Roger Mellie telly
(Roger Mellie, the man on the telly, is a strip cartoon character in the satirical magazine *Viz*, which began publication in 1979.)

Roger Moore door
(After the English actor (1927–2017) best known for playing James Bond from 1973 to 1985.)

Rogue and villain shilling
(First recorded in 1859, the term continued doing the rounds right up until the shilling – the equivalent of 5p – was withdrawn in 1971.)

Roller coaster toaster

Rolls-Royce choice
(An apt rhyme because if they could afford it, a lot of people would plump for a Rolls-Royce as their car of choice.)

Roman candles sandals
(Taken from the fireworks that have lit up 5 November for decades, and particularly fitting as sandals were the favoured footwear of the Romans.)

Romantic ballad salad

Ronnie Biggs digs (lodgings)
(A member of the gang who pulled off the Great Train Robbery of 1963 and then escaped after serving just fifteen months in jail.)

Rookery Nook book
(From the title of the 1923 novel written by Ben Travers (1886–1980) and subsequently adapted into a popular stage farce.)

Rory O'Moore door, floor
(A fictitious, all-purpose Irish character from the nineteenth century.)

Rosie Lee tea
(The identity of the original Rosie Lee remains a mystery but the rhyme bearing her name is believed to have originated around the time of the First World War.)

Rosie O'Grady's ladies' (toilet)

Round the houses trousers

Roy Hudds spuds (potatoes)
(After the veteran actor, comedian and expert on all things related to the music hall.)

Royal Mail bail

Rub-a-dub pub, sub (pay advance)
('Rub-a-dub' has been used as a rhyme for 'pub' since the early twentieth century and is generally abbreviated to 'rubber'.)

Ruby Murray curry
(Even though her heyday was the 1950s, Irish singer Ruby Murray (1935–96) was still fresh in the public's minds when the great curry boom hit Britain in the early seventies.)

Ruby red head

Rudolf Hess mess
(After Hitler's deputy (1894–1987) who flew solo to

Scotland in an attempt to negotiate peace with Britain and subsequenty became a prisoner of war.)

Ruin and spoil oil

Runner and rider cider

Rupert Bears flares (trousers), shares
(Created by English artist Mary Tourtel, Nutwood's most famous resident made his debut in a strip cartoon in the *Daily Express* in 1920.)

Rusty nail jail

S

Sad and sorry lorry

Safe and sound ground

Saint and sinner dinner
(A religious nineteenth-century term giving thanks to the Lord for food while at the same time hinting at the perils of gluttony.)

Salmon and trout gout, snout (tobacco), stout (beer)
('Snout' has been slang for 'tobacco' since the late nineteenth century and soon gave rise to the rhyme 'salmon and trout', or 'salmon' for short.)

Salvation Army barmy
(After the Christian charity founded by William Booth in London's East End in 1865.)

Samuel Pepys creeps
(From the celebrated London diarist (1633–1703), as in, 'This place gives me the Samuels.')

Sandy Powell towel

(A more palatable alternative to Enoch (see **Enoch Powell**) is this rhyme commemorating the red-haired, Yorkshire-born music-hall comedian (1898–1982).)

Santa's grotto blotto (drunk)
('Blotto' has been a slang term for 'very drunk' since the First World War.)

Satin and silk milk

Saucepan handle candle

Saucepan lid kid
(Although this can be used in the sense of 'to kid' meaning 'to fool', its most common form since the 1960s has been with reference to children.)

Sausage and mash cash, crash
(The rhyme is often shortened to 'sausage' and may have some connection with the phrase 'not a sausage' meaning 'absolutely nothing'.)

Sausage roll dole

Scooby-Doo clue
(After the clueless Great Dane who features in the Hanna-Barbera cartoons.)

Scotch eggs legs

Scotch pegs legs
(Dating from the mid-nineteenth century and usually abbreviated to 'scotches'.)

Scuba diver fiver

Sebastian Coes toes
(A relevant rhyme because few people could 'have it on their Sebs' (make a quick getaway) faster than the man who won 1,500 metres gold at both the 1980 and 1984 Olympics.)

Seek and search church

Semolina cleaner
(From the grim dessert that was a mainstay of school dinners in the 1950s.)

Sexton Blake fake
(Fictional English detective who made his debut in *The Halfpenny Marvel* magazine in 1893. Art forger Tom Keating called his forgeries his 'Sexton Blakes'.)

Shake and shiver river

Shepherd's pie sky
(Probably connected to the rhyme: 'Red sky at night shepherd's delight, Red sky in the morning shepherd's warning'.)

Sherbet Dab cab

Sherbet Dip kip

Shillings and pence sense

Shiny and bright all right

Shout and holler collar

Shovel and pick nick (prison)
(A reference to the tools once used by prisoners.)

Sighs and tears ears)

Silver and gold old

Silver spoon moon

Simply shocking stocking

Sinbad the Sailor tailor
(From the seafaring hero in *The Arabian Nights* stories.)

Sistine Chapel apple
(After the chapel in the papal palace in Rome's Vatican City, famous for its ornate ceiling by Michelangelo.)

Six and eight straight

Skin and blister sister
(A rhyme originating in the 1920s, as in, 'Is your skin and blister still going out with that geezer with the wonky minces?')

Sky rocket pocket
(First recorded in the nineteenth century and still heard today. The term is often shortened to 'sky'.)

Skylark park (a vehicle)

Skyscraper paper

Slap and tickle pickle
(A euphemism for foreplay, the 1979 song 'Slap And Tickle' by Squeeze contains the lines: 'Never chew a pickle, With a little slap and tickle'.)

Slug and snail fingernail

Smack in the eye pie
(Which could lead to some confusion if someone asks you, 'Do you want a smack in the eye?')

Smash and grab cab
(A thinly veiled accusation that taxi fares are daylight robbery.)

Smear and smudge judge

Smile and smirk work
(Often shortened to 'smile', as in, 'All smile and no Evelyn makes Jack a dull boy'.)

Snow and ice price

Snow Whites tights

Soap and lather father
(A late nineteenth-century rhyme mirroring Dad's morning shave.)

Soap and water daughter

Sodom and Gomorrah borrow ('borrer')
(According to the Book of Genesis, Sodom and Gomorrah were the two cities destroyed by God for their sinful reputations.)

Soldier bold cold
(An old military rhyme reminiscent of Private Pike in *Dad's Army* wrapped up in his woolly scarf on parade because his mum didn't want him to catch cold.)

Son and daughtered slaughtered (drunk)

Sooty and Sweep on the cheap
(Created by the late, great Harry Corbett (1918–89), Sooty and Sweep bestrode children's television for more than 50 years.)

Sorry and sad bad

Southend beach speech

Southend Piers ears

Spanish guitar cigar

Spanish waiter potato

Spare rib fib

Sparrow bow and arrow
(From the nursery rhyme 'Who Killed Cock Robin?' (see **Bow and arrow**).)

Spotted dick sick

Squad halt salt
(A military rhyme popular during the First World War.)

Squadron Leader Biggles giggles
(The daredevil British pilot and boys' own hero was created by author W. E. Johns in 1932 and went on to feature in nearly 100 books.)

St Louis blues shoes

Stage fright light (ale)

Stamford Bridge fridge
(In honour of the home ground of Chelsea Football Club.)

Stammer and stutter butter

Stan and Ollie brolly (umbrella)
(After comedy movie duo Stan Laurel (1890–1965) and Oliver Hardy (1892–1957).)

Stand at ease cheese

Stand to attention pension

Stars and Garters tomatoes
(After the title of the 1960s ITV variety show set in a London pub and hosted by Ray Martine and his pet mynah bird.)

Steam tug mug (fool)
(Invariably shortened to 'steamer', as in, 'Fancy falling for that old trick! What a steamer!')

Steely Dan tan
(After the New York jazz/rock founded by Donald Fagen and Walter Becker.)

Steve McQueens jeans
(In memory of the US movie star (1930–80), nicknamed the 'King of Cool'.)

Stevie Nicks flicks (cinema)
(After the American singer best known for her work with Fleetwood Mac in the 1970s.)

Stevie Wonder chunder (vomit), thunder
(The blind American singer/songwriter (born Steveland Judkins) had his first hit at thirteen.)

Stewed prune tune

Sticks and stones bones
(From the familiar playground rhyme: 'Sticks and stones may break my bones, but names will never hurt me'.)

Sticky toffee coffee

Stinging nettle kettle

Stone jug mug (fool)

Stop and start heart

Strawberry split git

Strawberry tart heart
(A puzzling rhyme until it is shortened to 'strawberry' and the visual connection becomes clear.)

String vest pest
(The string vest was invented in 1933 by Norwegian army commandant Henrik Brun who sewed together the first garment from old fishing nets.)

Struggle and strain train
(A rhyme that perfectly sums up rail travel in modern Britain.)

Stutter and stammer hammer

Sugar and spice nice
(From the old rhyme claiming that little girls are made of 'sugar and spice and all things nice'.)

Sunday roast post

Surrey Docks pox
(From the Thames-side area of Rotherhithe that served as a dockyard from 1696 to 1969.)

Swallow and sigh collar and tie
(Possibly based on what you might do if your tie is too tight.)

Swanee River liver

(The Suwanee River flows from Georgia to the Gulf of Mexico and in 1851 inspired Stephen C. Foster to write 'The Swanee River' (he misspelled the name).)

Swear and cuss bus

Sweaty sock Jock (Scotsman)

Sweeney Todd Flying Squad
(Sweeney Todd, the fictitious demon barber of Fleet Street, first appeared in print in 1846. In the early 1920s the *Daily Mail* gave the name Flying Squad to the fast response unit of the Metropolitan Police, and in 1975 ITV chose the slang term *The Sweeney* as the name for their hard-hitting cops and robbers series starring John Thaw.)

Swiss army knife wife

Syrup of fig wig
(A 1980s rhyme based on the dreaded laxative syrup of figs. The phrase is usually condensed to 'syrup'.)

T

Tapioca joker (cards)
(Tapioca is a starchy grain that was used to make a poor man's rice pudding in post-war Britain.)

Tate and Lyle style
(From the sugar company formed in 1921.)

Taxi rank bank

Tea and toast post
(A throwback to the time when the morning post in the UK used to arrive while you were having breakfast.)

Tea caddy Paddy (Irishman)

Tea leaf thief
(First heard around the start of the twentieth century and still in all-too-frequent use.)

Tennis racket jacket

Tent peg egg

These and those toes

Thick and thin chin, grin

This and that cat

Thomas Edison medicine
(The prolific Thomas Edison (1847–1931) held over 1,093 US patents, his most famous invention being the electric light bulb.)

Thomas Tilling shilling
(Thomas Tilling (1825–93) founded a transport company in 1846 and by the time of his death had a stable of 4,000 horses pulling buses across London.)

Tiddler's bait late
(Perhaps originating from the notion that a small boy fishing for tiddlers might be late home for his dinner.)

Tiddlywink drink
(Now shortened to 'tiddly', which has since become a familiar euphemism for 'slightly drunk'.)

Tilbury Docks socks
(After the port on the north bank of the Thames.)

Tin bath scarf
(Often shortened to 'tin', so that when venturing out into the cold you're advised to wear your 'tin and titfer' (see **Tit for tat**).)

Tin tack sack
(Dating back to the late nineteenth century, this has become the accepted rhyme for dismissal at work.)

Tin tank bank

Ting-a-ling ring

Tit for tat hat
(The phrase 'tit for tat' meaning 'retaliation' is said to originate from the sixteenth century 'tip for tap' referring to an exchange of blows.)

Toby jug mug (fool)
(First made by Staffordshire potters in the 1760s, a Toby jug usually depicts a man in a long coat and tricorn hat holding a mug of beer.)

Tod Sloan alone
(Tod Sloan (1874–1933) was an American jockey who suffered a fall from grace amid allegations that he had been betting on his own races. He died alone, giving rise to the expression 'on your tod'.)

Toilet roll dole

Tokyo Rose nose
(After the nickname given to Iva Toguri D'Aquino who tried to demoralise Allied troops by broadcasting Japanese propaganda during the Second World War.)

Tom and Dick sick
(The term 'Tom, Dick and Harry' meaning 'people in general' dates back to at least the nineteenth century.)

Tom and Jerry merry
(From the cartoon cat and mouse created by William Hanna and Joseph Barbera for MGM in 1940.)

Tom Sawyer lawyer
(From the boy hero of four novels by US writer Mark Twain, beginning with *The Adventures of Tom Sawyer* (1876).)

Tom Thumb rum
(After the hero in English folklore who was no bigger than his father's thumb.)

Tomato purée jury

Tomato sauce horse

Tomcat doormat

Tomfoolery jewellery
(In use since the 1930s, chiefly as underworld slang for stolen jewellery. It was soon shortened to 'tom'.)

Tommy Dodd God
(Nobody knows whether the Tommy Dodd in this nineteenth-century rhyme ever existed, which is probably why it appealed to atheists.)

Tommy guns the runs (diarrhoea)
(Inspired by the machine-gun fire with which a dose of diarrhoea splatters the toilet bowl.)

Tommy Steele jellied eel
(After Tommy Steele, the one-time merchant seaman who was launched as Britain's answer to Elvis in 1956.)

Tommy Trinder window
(With his pork-pie hat and catchphrase 'You lucky people', fast-talking, London-born comedian Tommy Trinder (1909–89) was one of Britain's most popular entertainers.)

Tommy Tucker sucker
(From the nursery rhyme – first published in 1829 – about orphan Little Tommy Tucker who sang for his supper.)

Tooting Bec peck (kiss)
(Based on the district of south London, as in, 'Go on, don't be shy – give her a Tooting on the cheek'.)

Top hat prat
(Surely a comment by the working classes on the vacuous toffs who turn up at places like Royal Ascot in their top hats.)

Town crier liar

Trafalgar Square chair

Treacle tart sweetheart
(More commonly shortened to 'treacle'.)

Treble chance dance
(A rhyme taken from the name of a multiple bet on the football pools.)

Trolley and tram ham
(A rhyme celebrating two old forms of London public transport – the tram and the trolleybus.)

Trombone phone
(This has continued to serve as a popular alternative to 'dog and bone' because of the link between the musical instrument and 'blower'.)

Trouble and strife wife
(Although the term implies marital discord it is generally used affectionately.)

Troubles and cares stairs

Tumble down the sink drink
(A nineteenth-century rhyme later shortened to 'tumble-down' or even 'tumble'.)

Turkish bath laugh

Turned and tossed lost

Turtle dove love

Turtle doves gloves
(First recorded in the 1850s and often abbreviated to 'turtles'.)

Twist and twirl girl

Two and eight state (mess)
(Originating in the 1930s, this rhyme usually refers to a nervous state but it can also apply to general untidiness.)

Two thirty dirty

U

Ugly sister blister
(From the Ugly Sisters who gave Cinderella such a hard time.)

Umbrella fella (boyfriend)

Uncle Ben ten
(Possibly derived from Uncle Ben's rice, first marketed in 1943.)

Uncle Bert shirt
(Usually shortened to 'uncle'.)

Uncle Billy chilly

Uncle Fred bread

Uncle Gus bus

Uncle Mac quack (doctor)
(Derek McCulloch – 'Uncle Mac' – (1897–1967) presented *Children's Hour* in the 1930s. The rhyme may originate from the fact that just as a 'quack' isn't a real doctor, so Uncle Mac wasn't your real uncle.)

Uncle Ned bed
(First recorded in the 1920s, this rhyme, too, can be shortened to 'uncle'.)

Uncle Reg veg
(Hence that Cockney favourite, 'Hands and feet and two Uncle Reg'.)

Uncle Sam lamb

Uncle Ted bed

Uncle Wilf the filth (police)

Uncle Willy silly

Uncles and aunts plants

Union Jack back
(Mentioning the flag of the United Kingdom often indicates a painful back, as in, 'I'm having real trouble with me Union just lately'.)

Up and down brown (ale)

Up and under thunder
(A Rugby League term much loved by colourful BBC commentator Eddie Waring (1910–86).)

V

Vanity Fair chair
(From the 1848 novel of that title by William Makepeace Thackeray (1811–63).)

Vera Lynn gin
(The 'Forces' Sweetheart' of the Second World War has become so associated with gin that it is frequently shortened to 'Vera'.)

Vincent Price ice
(After the US actor (1911–93), famous for his chilling roles in horror movies.)

Vincent van Gogh cough
(The Dutch painter (1853–90) was beset by depression, hallucinations and paranoia. In his later years he committed himself to a mental asylum and sliced off part of his left ear.)

Von Trapp crap
(The Austrian von Trapp family were a group of singers whose escape from the Nazis inspired *The Sound of Music*.)

Walnut Whip kip
(For the uninitiated a Walnut Whip is a chocolate cone with a whipped vanilla fondant filling and a walnut on top.)

Walter Mitty kitty
(Based on the fictional character in James Thurber's story *The Secret Life of Walter Mitty*, first published in 1939. As in, 'How much bread is left in the Walter?')

Wanstead Flats spats
(A late nineteenth-century rhyme from the days when spats – short fabric covers that were worn on the lower leg to protect the wearer's shoes from mud – were the height of fashion.)

Watch and chain brain
(This rhyme related to intelligence – or lack of it – leading to remarks such as, 'You'll have to excuse him, his watch is a bit slow'.)

Water bottle throttle

Watford Gap slap
(After the geographical break in the hills in Northamptonshire. Used as in, 'If he carries on like that he's going to get a Watford Gap'.)

Weasel and stoat coat
(This familiar rhyme may stem from the fact that both animals are renowned for their fine coats.)

Weaver's chair prayer

Wee Georgie Wood good
(Commemorating the 4ft 9in British music-hall comedian (1894–1979) who spent much of his career playing children.)

Weeping willow pillow

West Ham Reserves nerves
(After the East End football club and usually shortened to 'West Hams'.)

Westminster Abbey cabbie, shabby

Whip and top strop
(From the child's toy of the nineteenth and early twentieth centuries. The rhyme is often shortened to 'whip', as in, 'Your love and kisses is in a bit of a whip today'.)

Whisky and soda Skoda

Whistle and flute suit
(Usually shortened to 'whistle', as in, 'I've only gone and spilt rocking horse down me new whistle!')

Whistle and toot loot

White Cliffs of Dover over
('Over' and 'Dover' have been a rhyming couple since Vera Lynn's 1940s stirring rendition of 'There'll Be Bluebirds Over The White Cliffs of Dover'.)

White mice ice
(As in the unlikely request, 'Do you want white mice in your Scotch?')

Whitechapel apple
(From the district's long-standing association with Spitalfields fruit and vegetable market until it moved to a new location in 1991.)

Wicked rumours bloomers (knickers)

Widow Twankey hanky (handkerchief)
(After the name of the comic washerwoman – normally played by a man – in the pantomime *Aladdin*.)

Wilbur Wright flight
(The American Wright brothers Wilbur (1867–1912) and Orville (1871–1948) were the pioneers of aviation who, in 1903, made the first powered flight in an aeroplane.)

Wild West vest

Wilfrid Brambell gamble
(Irish actor (1912–85) who played rag and bone man Albert Steptoe in the classic TV sitcom *Steptoe and Son*.)

Will o' the wisps crisps

William Joyce voice
(Alias 'Lord Haw Haw', William Joyce (1906–46) possessed the most hated voice in the Second World War as he broadcast Nazi propaganda over British airwaves.)

William Tell smell
(Based on the fourteenth-century Swiss folk hero.)

Wilson Pickett ticket
(A rhyme taken from the name of the US soul singer (1941–2006).)

Wind and kite web site

Winnie the Pooh shoe
(Created by English author A. A. Milne (1882–1956), the lovable bear with a taste for honey first appeared in book form in 1926.)

Wooden pews news

Wooden plank Yank (American)

Woolwich and Greenwich spinach
(From two districts of south-east London where the second is pronounced 'Grinidge'.)

Working classes glasses

Worms and snails fingernails

Worzel Gummidge rummage
(The talking scarecrow made his debut in print in 1936.)

Wyatt Earp burp

(After the Wild West marshal (1848–1929) who kept law and order in Dodge City and participated in the infamous Gunfight at the OK Corral in 1881.)

XYZ

Yankee Doodles noodles
(See **Macaroni**)

Yarmouth bloater motor
(From the Norfolk fishing port of Great Yarmouth, renowned for its smoked fish, a UK bloater being a smoked herring.)

Yellow silk milk

Yorkshire Tyke mike (microphone)
('Tyke' is slang for a Yorkshireman.)

You and me tea

You must crust
(A simple rhyme from post-war Britain urging children to eat the crusts off their bread.)

Yours and ours flowers

English to Cockney

A

Advice lump of ice

Ale Daily Mail

All nighter jet fighter

All right shiny and bright

Alone (On your own) Darby and Joan, Tod Sloan, Jack Jones

Appendix Jimi Hendrix

Apple Sistine Chapel, Whitechapel

Arm Chalk Farm, false alarm, lucky charm

Army daft and barmy

Aunt garden plant

B

Back Penny Black, Union Jack

Bad Jack the Lad, sorry and sad

Bail Royal Mail

Baked beans kings and queens

Baker Long Acre

Balti Basil Fawlty

Banana Gertie Gitana

Bank Armitage Shank, cab rank, fish and tank, iron tank, rattle and clank, taxi rank, tin tank

Bar Jack tar, Jean Michel Jarre

Barber Dover harbour

Barmy Dad's Army, Monty's army, Salvation Army

Barrow cock sparrow

Basin Charlie Mason, Fortnum & Mason

Bath hat and scarf

Battery charm and flattery

Batty Carlo Gatti

Beak (see **Magistrate**)

Beard strange and weird

Bed Uncle Ned, Uncle Ted

Beef itchy teeth

Beer (Bitter, Bottle of Bass, Brown (ale), Guinness, Lager, Light (ale), Mild, Stout) Christmas cheer, pig's ear, apple fritter, kitty litter, laugh and titter, up and down, photo finish, Forsyte Saga, day and night, stage fright, salmon and trout

Beginner Lilley and Skinner

Believe Adam and Eve

Bell Little Nell

Belly Auntie Nelly, Darby Kelly, George Melly, New Delhi

Berk Charlie Smirke

Best Mae West

Bet deep in debt

Big Porky Pig

Bigot Lester Piggott

Bike Dick Van Dyke

Bill Muswell Hill

Bingo George and Ringo

Bitter (see **Beer**)

Black coalman's sack

Blade (knife) First aid

Blind Golden Hind

Blister Ugly sister

Bloke heap of coke

Bloomers (see **Knickers**)

Blotto (see **Drunk**)

Blower (see **Phone**)

Boat frog in the throat, hat and coat

Bob (see **Shilling**)

Body Big Ears and Noddy

Bog (toilet) (Khazi, Throne) Captain's log, Kermit the frog, Frank Zappa, Ilie Nastase, rag and bone

Bogey Jimmy Logie, old fogey

Boil (spot) Bodie and Doyle, Conan Doyle

Bones sticks and stones

Bonkers marbles and conkers

Book Captain Hook, fish hook, Rookery Nook

Bookie cream cookie

Boots daisy roots, King Canutes

Booze pick and choose, River Ouse

Boozer (see Pub)

Borrow Sodom and Gomorrah

Boss dead loss

Bottle Aristotle, Gerry Cottle

Bottle of Bass (see Beer)

Bounce (a cheque) half-ounce

Bouncer (doorman) half-ouncer

Bow and arrow sparrow

Bowler (hat) bottle of cola

Box (theatre) Charles James Fox

Boy pride and joy, Rob Roy

Boy Scout brussel sprout

Bra ooh la la

Braces airs and graces, Ascot Races

Brain down the drain, watch and chain

Brakes Charlie Drakes

Brandy fine and dandy, Mahatma Gandhi

Brat Jack Sprat

Bread needle and thread, Uncle Fred

Breath life and death

Brick Dublin trick

Bride fat and wide, mother's pride

Broke (penniless) coals and coke

Brolly (see **Umbrella**)

Broom bride and groom

Brother manhole cover

Brown (ale) (see **Beer**)

Brown (halfpenny) Camden Town

Brown (snooker ball) half a crown

Bunion pickled onion

Burp Wyatt Earp

Bus don't make a fuss, swear and cuss, Uncle Gus

Butter mutter and stutter, stammer and stutter

Button Len Hutton

C

Cab (Taxi) flounder and dab, Sherbet Dab, smash and grab, Joe Baksi

Cabbie Westminster Abbey

Cadge coat and badge

Café Colonel Gaddafi

Cake give and take

Can (safe) Peter Pan

Cancel Nigel Mansell

Candle saucepan handle

Cans (headphones) Desperate Dans

Cap game of nap

Car (Motor) jamjar, haddock and bloater, Yarmouth bloater

Cards (playing) Coldstream Guards

Carrots Polly parrots

Cash (Readies) Arthur Ashe, bangers and mash, pie and mash, sausage and mash, Nelson Eddys

Cat cooking fat, this and that

Ceiling funny feeling

Cell (prison) flowery dell

Chair here and there, lion's lair, Lionel Blair, Trafalgar Square, Vanity Fair

Chalk Duke of York, Lambeth Walk

Chancer ballet dancer

Change (money) rifle range

Charmer Jeffrey Dahmer

Chat chew the fat

Cheek (nerve) hide and seek

Cheeky cockaleekie

Cheese balmy breeze, John Cleese, stand at ease

Cheque chicken's neck, goose's neck, Jeff Beck, nervous wreck, pain in the neck

Chest bird's nest, east and west, Mae West

Chief corned beef

Chill Jimmy Hill

Chilly Uncle Billy

Chin Andy McGinn, Errol Flynn, Gilbey's gin, thick and thin

Chip lucky dip

Chips jockeys' whips

Choice Rolls-Royce

Choker Bram Stoker

Chum Fruit Gum

Chunder (see **Vomit**)

Church left in the lurch, seek and search

Cider runner and rider, Shaun Ryder

Cigar La-di-da, Spanish guitar

Cigarette lighter kung fu fighter

Clanger coat hanger

Claret (blood) boiled beef and carrot

Cleaner semolina

Clink (see **Jail**)

Clock dickory dock

Closed doublet and hosed

Clothes line grape vine

Clown Charlie Brown

Clue didgeridoo, pot of glue, Scooby-Doo

Coal merry old soul

Coat all afloat, bucket afloat, Dover boat, nanny goat, pound note, Quaker Oat, weasel and stoat

Cockney rhyming slang Chitty Chitty Bang Bang

Cod Richard Todd

Coffee Everton toffee, sticky toffee

Cold Cheltenham Gold, potatoes in the mould, soldier bold

Collar Oxford scholar, shout and holler

Collar and tie swallow and sigh

Comb garden gnomee

Concertina constant screamer

Conk (see **Nose**)

Cook babbling brook

Cop (police officer) (Copper, Filth) lemon drop, pork chop, bottle and stopper, clodhopper, grasshopper, Uncle Wilf

Copper (see **Cop**)

Cords (corduroy trousers) House of Lords

Corner Johnny Horner

Cough horse and trough, on and off, Vincent van Gogh

Cousin baker's dozen

Cow Chairman Mao

Coward Frankie Howerd

Cramp rising damp

Crash sausage and mash

Creeps Samuel Pepys

Crime lemon and lime

Cripple raspberry ripple

Crisps will o' the wisps

Crook babbling brook

Crust you must

Cup dog and pup

Cupboard Mother Hubbard

Curry Ruby Murray

Curtains Richard Burtons

D

Daft fore and aft

Dance kick and prance, treble chance

Darts horses and carts

Daughter bottle of water, bricks and mortar, soap and water

Dead brown bread, gone to bed

Deal jellied eel

Denial River Nile

Dense garden fence

Dice cats and mice

Diesel pop goes the weasel

Diet Brixton riot, peace and quiet

Digs (lodgings) Ronnie Biggs

Dinner Michael Winner, saint and sinner

Dirty hundred to thirty, two thirty

Doddle Glenn Hoddle

Dog London fog

Dogs (greyhound racing) cherry hogs

Dole (Giro) jam roll, Nat King Cole, Old King Cole, rock 'n' roll, sausage roll, toilet roll, Night Boat to Cairo

Dollar Oxford scholar

Door George Bernard Shaw, Roger Moore, Rory O'Moore

Doormat tomcat

Dosh (see **Money**)

Double (in darts) rasher and bubble

Dough (see **Money**)

Dozen country cousin

Draught George Raft

Drawers (see **Knickers**)

Dreams custard creams

Dress mustard and cress

Drill Benny Hill

Drink Engelbert Humperdinck, kitchen sink, tiddlywink, tumble down the sink

Drunk (Blotto, Plastered, Slaughtered, Smashed, Tiddly) elephant's trunk, Mickey Monk, Santa's Grotto, booed and hissed, Brahms and Liszt, fog and mist, Gorillas in the Mist, hand and fist, Oliver Twist, Scotch mist, lord and mastered, son and daughtered, pebble-dashed, Bo Diddley

E

Ear bottle of beer, glass of beer

Earner, nice little Bunsen burner

Ears King Lears, lords and peers, sighs and tears, Southend Piers

Easy ham and cheesy, lemon squeezy

Egg borrow and beg, tent peg

Eight garden gate

Epsom races airs and graces

Evens (betting odds) Major Stevens

Eyes mince pies

F

Face Boat Race, Chevy Chase, fillet of plaice, kipper and plaice, Peyton Place

Facts brass tacks

Fag (cigarette) (Smoke, Woods (Woodbines)) Harry Wragg, jet lag, oily rag, puff and drag, laugh and joke, do me goods

Fags (cigarettes) Oxford bags

Fake Sexton Blake

Fare grey mare

Fart raspberry tart

Fat Jack Sprat

Father soap and lather

Favour cheesy Quaver

Feel orange peel

Feet dog's meat, plates of meat

Fella (boyfriend) umbrella

Fever Robinson and Cleaver

Fib spare rib

Fiddle hey diddle diddle

Fight left and right, read and write

Filth (see Cop)

Fine (penalty) bottle of wine

Fingernail slug and snail

Fingernails worms and snails

Fingers bell ringers

Fire Anna Maria, Black Maria

First (degree result) Geoff Hurst, Pattie Hearst, raging thirst

Fish Lillian Gish

Five man alive

Fiver deep sea diver, Lady Godiva, scuba diver

Flares (trousers) Dan Dares, Lionel Blairs, Rupert Bears

Flicks (cinema) Stevie Nicks

Flies Morecambe and Wise

Flight Wilbur Wright

Floor Mrs Moore, Rory O'Moore

Flowers April showers, early hours, yours and ours

Flu inky blue

Flutter (bet) grumble and mutter

Flying Squad Sweeney Todd

Fob (watch) kettle and hob

Food in the mood

Fool garden tool

Foot chimney and soot

Football pools April Fools

Foreman Joe O'Gorman

Fork Duke of York, roast pork

Four knock at the door

French, the bloody muddy trench

Fridge London Bridge, Stamford Bridge

Friend Mile End

Front (nerve) James Hunt

Funnel Blackwall Tunnel

G

Gal (see **Girl**)

Gamble Wilfrid Brambell

Garage horse and carriage

Garden Dolly Varden

Geezer fridge freezer, Julius Caesar, lemon squeezer

Ghost pillar and post

Giggles Squadron Leader Biggles

Gin Brian O'Linn, needle and pin, Nell Gwynn, Vera Lynn

Gin and tonic philharmonic

Girl (Gal) ivory pearl, mother of pearl, ribbon and curl, twist and twirl, Pall Mall

Giro (see **Dole**)

Git strawberry split

Glasses (Specs) working classes

Gloves turtle doves

God Tommy Dodd

Goggle box (see **Telly**)

Good Robin Hood, Wee Georgie Wood

Gout in and out, salmon and trout

Grand (£1,000) bag of sand

Grass old iron and brass

Grass (police informant) (Nark) car park, grass in the park, Noah's Ark

Gravy Army and Navy

Greens (vegetables) has beens, Nellie Deans

Grey night and day

Grief Omar Sharif

Grin thick and thin

Ground safe and sound

Grumble rhubarb crumble

Guinness (see **Beer**)

Gut (stomach) Limehouse Cut

Guts fruit and nuts

Gutter bread and butter

Haddock Bessie Braddock, Fanny Cradock

Hair Barnet Fair, Biffo the Bear, Fred Astaire, Alf Garnett (barnet)

Half (pint of beer) cow and calf

Ham trolley and tram

Hammer stutter and stammer

Hand brass band, German band

Hands Margate sands

Handy Jack and Dandy

Hanky (handkerchief) Widow Twankey

Hard bread and lard, Marquis de Sade

Hat (Tile) ball and bat, tit for tat, penny-a-mile

Head ball of lead, crust of bread, Judge Dredd, loaf of bread, lump of lead, ruby red

Head (of family) daily bread

Heart jam tart, stop and start, strawberry tart

Hell ding dong bell

Hill Jack and Jill

Hole drum roll

Home gates of Rome

Honda Henry Fonda

Honours Jimmy Connors

Hooter (see **Nose**)

Horse bottle of sauce, tomato sauce

Hot Alan Knott, peas in the pot

House cat and mouse, Mickey Mouse

Huff cream puff

Hump (anger) petrol pump

I

Ice Vincent Price, white mice

Itch Little Tich

J

Jacket fag packet, tennis racket

Jail (Clink, Nick, Slammer) bucket and pail, ginger ale, moan and wail, rusty nail, kitchen sink, shovel and pick

Jam baby's pram

Jeans baked beans, Bethnal Greens, Dixie Deans, Steve McQueens

Jellied eel Tommy Steele

Jewellery tomfoolery

Jive duck and dive

Job corn on the cob, couple of bob, knocker and knob

Jock (Scotsman) sweaty sock

Johnny (condom) Reggie and Ronnie

Joke can of Coke, egg yolk

Joker (playing cards) tapioca

Judge Barnaby Rudge, chocolate fudge, inky smudge, smear and smudge

Jury tomato purée

K

Karaoke hokey cokey

Keen James Dean

Kettle Hansel and Gretel, stinging nettle

Key Bruce Lee

Keys Cheddar cheese, dancing fleas, honey bees, knobbly knees

Khazi (see **Bog**)

Kid (child) dustbin lid, God forbid, saucepan lid

King (playing cards) Highland fling

Kip (sleep) jockey's whip, lucky dip, Sherbet Dip, Walnut Whip

Kipper Jack the Ripper

Kiss heavenly bliss, hit and miss

Kitty Walter Mitty

Knackered cream crackered

Knees biscuits and cheese, chips and peas

Knickers (Bloomers, Drawers) Alan Whickers, Bill Stickers, wicked rumours, Diana Dors

Knife drum and fife, man and wife

Kraut (German) lager lout

L

Laces dirty faces

Ladder Blackadder

Ladies' (toilet) Rosie O'Grady's

Lager (see Beer)

Lamb Uncle Sam

Lark Joan of Arc, Noah's Ark

Late tiddler's bait

Later alligator

Lather (state) how's your father?

Laugh giraffe, Turkish bath

Lawyer Tom Sawyer

Lazy Gert and Daisy

Legs (Pins) bacon and eggs, clothes pegs, cribbage pegs, pin pegs, Scotch eggs, Scotch pegs, Rin Tin Tins

Leicester Square Euan Blair

Liar Bob Cryer, deep fat fryer, Dunlop tyre, town crier

Lie cherry pie, collar and tie

Lies pork pies

Light (ale) (see **Beer**)

Lips apple pips

Lisp Quentin Crisp

Liver bow and quiver, Swanee River

Loan shark Cutty Sark

Lodger Artful Dodger, Jolly Roger

Look butcher's hook, Captain Cook

Loon Keith Moon

Loose Mother Goose

Loot whistle and toot

Lorry sad and sorry

Lost turned and tossed

Love turtle dove

Lunch kidney punch

M

Mad Mum and Dad

Magistrate (Beak) garden gate, bubble and squeak

Married cash and carried

Mason David Jason, Larry Grayson

Match down the hatch

Matches cuts and scratches

Mate china plate, dinner plate

Meat hands and feet

Medicine Thomas Edison

Mental chicken oriental, Radio Rental

Merry Tom and Jerry

Mess Eliot Ness, Rudolf Hess

Mike (microphone) Yorkshire Tyke

Mild (see **Beer**)

Milk Acker Bilk, lady in silk, satin and silk, yellow silk

Mind bacon rind

Missus (see **Wife**)

Mobi (mobile phone) Obi-Wan Kenobi

Money (Dosh, Dough, Wad, Wedge) bees and honey, bread and honey, Bugs Bunny, Easter bunny, Rogan Josh, Ken Dodd, Percy Sledge

Moody Punch and Judy

Moon silver spoon

Motor (see **Car**)

Moustache dot and dash

Mouth north and south

Muddle kiss and cuddle

Mug (drinking) barge and tug

Mug (fool) steam tug, stone jug, Toby jug

Mum finger and thumb

Murder iron girder

Muscles greens and brussels

Mutton Billy Button

N

Nag paper bag

Nail monkey's tail

Nark (police informant) (see **Grass**)

Neck bushel and peck

Neighbour hard labour

Nerves West Ham Reserves

News bottle of booze, wooden pews

Newspaper linen draper

Nice sugar and spice

Nick (see **Jail**)

Night black and white

Nightie God almighty

Nine Brighton line

Nipper (child) fly tipper

Noise box of toys, girls and boys

Noodles Yankee Doodles

Nose (Conk, Hooter) doublet and hose, fireman's hose, I suppose, Tokyo Rose, glass of plonk, pea shooter

Nun hot cross bun

Nutter brandy butter, bread and butter, peanut butter

Nutty chip butty

Oats John O'Groats

Oil ruin and spoil

Old silver and gold

Old man (husband or father) frying pan, pot and pan

On the cheap Sooty and Sweep

On the labour (exchange) beggar my neighbour

On the pull John Bull

On your own (see **Alone**)

One buttered bun

Onions corns and bunions

Organ (musical) Captain Morgan

Over White Cliffs of Dover

P

Paddy (Irishman) goodie and baddie, tea caddy

Pain Hanger Lane, Michael Caine

Pants Adam Ants, fleas and ants, Pirates of Penzance

Paper skyscraper

Park Noah's Ark

Park (a vehicle) skylark

Parole jam roll

Party hale and hearty, Moriarty

Pathetic Charlton Athletic

Peck (kiss) Tooting Bec

Pen Dirty Den

Pension stand to attention

Pepper dirty leper

Pest string vest

Phone (Blower) Darby and Joan, dog and bone, eau de Cologne, jelly bone, trombone, Percy Thrower

Photo kipper and bloater

Piano Joanna

Pick (tool) Paddy and Mick

Pickle slap and tickle

Pickles Harvey Nichols

Pie Captain Bligh, smack in the eye

Pillow weeping willow

Pinch (steal) half-inch

Pink (snooker ball) rinky dink

Pins (see **Legs**)

Pipe cherry ripe

Pitch hedge and ditch

Pizza Mona Lisa

Plan Jackie Chan, Manfred Mann

Plants uncles and aunts

Plastered (see **Drunk**)

Plate Alexander the Great, Pearly Gate

Play (theatrical) Evelyn Laye

Please hairy knees

Plug little brown jug

Pocket chain and locket, Davy Crockett, Lucy Locket, penny locket, sky rocket

Poker jolly joker

Pong (see **Smell**)

Pony (£25) macaroni

Poor on the floor

Pope bar of soap

Port (wine) didn't ought

Poser bulldozer, Carl Rosa

Post (mail) beans on toast, Holy Ghost, Sunday roast, tea and toast

Potato (Spuds) Spanish waiter, Roy Hudds

Pound Huckleberry Hound, lost and found, merry-go-round

Pox boots and socks, cardboard box, Dairy Box, East India Docks, Goldilocks, Jack in the box, Surrey Docks

Prat mackerel and sprat, top hat

Prayer chocolate éclair, weaver's chair

Price snow and ice

Priest bag of yeast

Pub (Boozer) nuclear sub, rub-a-dub, battle cruiser

Puff Nellie Duff

Pull (chat up) cotton wool

Punter Billy Bunter

Purse doctor and nurse

Pyjamas panoramas

Q

Quack (doctor) Uncle Mac

Queen (Elizabeth II) baked bean

Quid (£1) bin lid

R

Rain pleasure and pain

Rave Comedy Dave

Raver cheesy Quaver

Razor Frankie Fraser

Readies (see **Cash**)

Red (snooker ball) bald head

Rent Duke of Kent

Ride Charlie Pride

Right harbour light, Isle of Wight

Ring (jewellery) Highland fling, ting-a-ling

Rip acid trip

River shake and shiver

Road frog and toad

Room bride and groom

Rough Mickey Duff

Round (of drinks) hare and hound

Row (argument) bull and cow, pantomime cow

Rum finger and thumb, Tom Thumb

Rummage Worzel Gummidge

Runs (see **Diarrhoea**)

S

Sack last card of the pack, Roberta Flack, tin tack

Sad Alan Ladd

Salad romantic ballad

Saloon bar balloon car

Salt Earls Court, squad halt

Sandals Roman candles

Sauce Air Force, rocking horse

Saucer Geoffrey Chaucer

Saveloy Myrna Loy

Saw bear's paw, mother-in-law

Say so cocoa

Scar Mars bar

Scarf centre-half, half and half, tin bath

Scary Bloody Mary

Score (£20) Bobby Moore

Scotch (see **Whisky**)

Scouser Mickey Mouser

Sea housemaid's knee

Sense pounds and pence, shillings and pence

Shabby Westminster Abbey

Shades (sunglasses) Jack of Spades

Shakes, the Hattie Jacques

Shandy Andy Pandy, Beano and Dandy

Shares Rupert Bears

Shave Chas and Dave, Mexican wave, ocean wave, rant and rave

Shilling (Bob) rogue and villain, Thomas Tilling, doorknob

Shiner (black eye) Morris Minor, ocean liner

Ship halfpenny dip

Shirt dicky dirt, Uncle Bert

Shoe Winnie the Pooh

Shoes five to twos, Looby Loos, ones and twos, rhythm and blues, St Louis blues

Shooter (gun) Phil the Fluter

Shop lollipop, Mrs Mopp

Short (drink) magistrate's court

Shoulders Noddy Holders, rocks and boulders

Shout brussel sprout

Shovel Lord Lovell

Shower Blackpool Tower, Eiffel Tower

Shrimp Colonel Blimp

Shut Jabba the Hutt

Sick Moby Dick, spotted dick, Tom and Dick

Silly daffadown dilly, Piccadilly, Uncle Willy

Singer mangle and wringer

Sister skin and blister

Six pick up sticks

Sixty-six clickety click

Skint Bernie Flint, boracic lint, Murray mint, Polo mint

Skiver backseat driver

Skoda whisky and soda

Sky shepherd's pie

Slammer (see **Jail**)

Slap brandy snap, Watford Gap

Slaughtered (see **Drunk**)

Sleep Bo Peep

Slippers big dippers, Jack the Rippers, pair of kippers

Smart lemon tart

Smashed (see **Drunk**)

Smell (Pong, Stink, Whiff) heaven and hell, William Tell, Anna May Wong, pen and ink, Jimmy Cliff

Smoke cough and choke

Smoke (cigarette) (see **Fag**)

Smoke (London) old oak

Snake George Blake

Sneeze bread and cheese

Snore lion's roar

Snout (see **Tobacco**)

Snow buck and doe

Snuff blindman's buff

Soap Band of Hope, Bob Hope

Socks almond rocks, diamond rocks, Tilbury Docks

Son bath bun, currant bun

Song ding dong

Sores Dudley Moores

Soup bowl the hoop, loop the loop

Sparrow bow and arrow

Spats Wanstead Flats

Speak bubble and squeak

Specs (see **Glasses**)

Speech Southend beach

Spinach Woolwich and Greenwich

Splinter Harold Pinter

Spoon blue moon, Lorna Doone, man on the moon

Spot jelly tot, Randolph Scott

Spouse boiler house

Spuds (see **Potato**)

Squatter pig's trotter

Squeal (inform on) conger eel

Stab doner kebab

Stain Cynthia Payne, Michael Caine

Stairs apples and pears, dancing bears, troubles and cares

Starvin' Hank Marvin

State (mess) two and eight

Station poor relation

Stays (corset) Bryant and Mays

Steak Joe Blake

Steak and kidney Kate and Sidney

Stew Battle of Waterloo

Stink (see Smell)

Stocking reeling and rocking, simply shocking

Stolen goods Little Red Riding Hoods

Stool Peter O'Toole

Stop thief hot beef

Story Jackanory

Stout (see Beer)

Straight six and eight

Stranger Glasgow Ranger, Queens Park Ranger

Street ain't it a treat, field of wheat

Stretch Jack Ketch

Strides (see Trousers)

Stripper herring and kipper

Strop whip and top

Stunner air gunner

Style Tate and Lyle

Sub (pay advance) rub-a-dub

Sucker Tommy Tucker

Suit bowl of fruit, whistle and flute

Sulk Incredible Hulk

Sun bath bun, currant bun

Sun (newspaper) currant bun

Suspenders no surrenders

Swear Lord Mayor, rip and tear

Sweetheart treacle tart

T

Table Betty Grable, Cain and Abel

Taff (Welshman) riff raff

Tail alderman's nail

Tailor Sinbad the Sailor

Tale Daily Mail, Newgate Gaol

Talk Duke of York, rabbit and pork

Talker Johnnie Walker, Murray Walker

Tan Charlie Chan, Steely Dan

Tanner (sixpence) lord of the manor

Tax Ajax, bees' wax

Taxi (see Cab)

Tea Rosie Lee, you and me

Teeth Edward Heath, Hampstead Heath, roast beef

Telly (Goggle box) custard and jelly, Marie Corelli Roger Mellie, Nervo and Knox

Ten Big Ben, Bill and Ben, cock and hen, Uncle Ben

Thick (stupid) king dick, Paddy and Mick, Queen Vic

Thief leg of beef, tea leaf

Thieves Jimmy Greaves

Thin needle and pin

Third (degree result) Douglas Hurd

Thirst Geoff Hurst

Thirty Burlington Bertie

Throat nanny goat

Throne (see **Bog**)

Throttle water bottle

Thumb Jamaica rum

Thunder Stevie Wonder, up and under

Ticket bat and wicket, Wilson Pickett

Tiddly (see **Drunk**)

Tie Peckham Rye

Tights fly-by-nights, Snow Whites

Tile (see **Hat**)

Till Benny Hill

Time Harry Lime, lager and lime

Time (prison sentence) birdlime

Times (newspaper) nursery rhymes

Tired barb-wired

Toast Holy Ghost, Mickie Most

Toaster roller coaster

Tobacco (Snout) Oi Jimmy Knacker, salmon and trout

Toes buttons and bows, Sebastian Coes, these and those

Tomatoes Stars and Garters

Tools April Fools, Crown Jewels

Tote canal boat

Totty Bruno N'Gotty

Towel Enoch Powell, mortar and trowel, Sandy Powell

Toy girl and boy

Traffic warden Gay Gordon

Train hail and rain, John Wayne, struggle and strain

Tram baa lamb, bread and jam

Tramp halfpenny stamp, hurricane lamp, paraffin lamp

Trousers (Strides) Callard & Bowsers, council houses, round the houses, Herbie Hides, Jekyll and Hydes

Trowel Baden-Powell, bark and growl

True Irish stew

Truth Maud and Ruth

Tune stewed prune

Turk Captain Kirk

Turkey Pinky and Perky

Twenty Horn of Plenty

Twig (understand) earwig

Twins needles and pins

2:1 (degree result) Attila the Hun

2:2 (degree result) Desmond (Tutu)

Tyre Billy Liar

U

Umbrella (Brolly) Auntie Ella, Stan and Ollie
Undertaker overcoat maker

V

Van Peter Pan
Veg Uncle Reg
Very best John West
Vest east and west, Wild West
Vicar half a nicker, pie and liquor
Villain Bob Dylan, Harold Macmillan
Vin blanc (white wine) plinkety plonk
Voddie (vodka) Bill Oddie
Voice William Joyce

W

Wad (see Money)
Wages greengages, rock of ages
Waistcoat Charlie Prescott

Waiter cheese grater, hot potato

Wales Canterbury Tales

Walk ball of chalk, Duke of York

Watch bottle of Scotch

Water didn't oughta, fisherman's daughter

Weather hat and feather

Web site wind and kite

Wedge (see **Money**)

Weight Alfred the Great, pieces of eight

West (End of London) jacket and vest

Wheels (transport) jellied eels

Whiff (see **Smell**)

Whiskers hammer and discus

Whisky (Scotch) gay and frisky, gold watch, pimple and. blotch

Whistle Partick Thistle

Wife (Missus) bread knife, carving knife, drum and fife, Duchess of Fife, Swiss army knife, trouble and strife, hugs and kisses, love and kisses

Wig guinea pig, Irish jig, syrup of fig

Win nose and chin

Window burnt cinder, Tommy Trinder

Wine River Tyne

Winkles Granny's wrinkles

Winner chicken dinner, hot dinner

Wishes pots and dishes

Woman gooseberry puddin'

Woods (Woodbines) (see **Fag**)

Word dicky bird

Work Captain Kirk, smile and smirk

Wrong Pete Tong

XYZ

Yank (American) board and plank, wooden plank

Yanks (Americans) ham shanks

Years donkey's ears

Yes Brown Bess

9 10 8

Published in 2019 by Pop Press, an imprint of Ebury Publishing

20 Vauxhall Bridge Road,
London SW1V 2SA

Pop Press is part of Penguin Random House group of companies
whose addresses can be found at global.penguinrandomhouse.com

Text © Geoff Tibballs 2019

Geoff Tibballs has asserted his right to be identified
as the author of this Work in accordance with the
Copyright, Designs and Patents Act 1988

First published in 2008 by Ebury Press.

www.penguin.co.uk

A CIP catalogue record for this book
is available from the British Library

ISBN 9781529103922

Designed by seagulls.net
Printed and bound in Great Britain by Clays Ltd, Elcograf S.p.A.

Penguin Random House is committed to a sustainable future for our
business, our readers and our planet. This book is made from Forest
Stewardship Council® certified paper.